THE ENERGY OF YOU

A Journey to Unlock Your Inner Wisdom and Live with Purpose

NISHA PURUSHOTHAMAN

Clever Fox® PUBLISHING
Chennai • Bangalore

CLEVER FOX PUBLISHING
Chennai, India

Published by CLEVER FOX PUBLISHING 2025

ISBN: 978-93-6707-762-7

CONTENTS

INTRODUCTION

Osho (the guru from the Netflix show Wild Wild Country - dubious maybe, but he said some really wise things!) once said, "Doubt is an inner potential; it is the only way a person will be able to inquire, search, and seek." He encouraged us not to suppress doubt but to embrace it, nurture it, and let it fuel a great quest. As a lifelong skeptic, I took this to heart. Doubt became my guide, sparking questions that unraveled my understanding of life and led me deeper into its mysteries. With every answer I found, new doubts emerged, and with them, fresh insights. This book, The Energy of You, is the harvest of that relentless seeking—a journey born from curiosity and a hunger to explore the unseen threads that connect us all.

This path wouldn't have unfolded without the people and experiences that shaped it. My parents laid the foundation, unknowingly setting me on this course. My siblings, family, and friends offered both challenges and support, pushing me forward. Even my ex-husband played a role, complex as it was, in this unfolding story. But above all, my children—Arjun, Varun, and Rajiv—have been my greatest teachers. Through them, I glimpsed something rare and transformative: unconditional love.

We're often told that all love comes with conditions—even a parent's love for their child—because expectations inevitably slip in. Yet, there are moments, fleeting and pure, when you look at your child and feel an overwhelming rush of love, free from pride or attachment. For just a second, it's love without strings—before it shifts into thoughts like, "What a wonderful kid I've raised," or "How can I hold onto this feeling?" It's easier to touch this purity with children than with adults, but those brief seconds reveal something profound. Unconditional love isn't just selflessness or sacrifice—it's the recognition that we are all connected. It is that yearning to be connected with that "whole" again. And to love another is really to love ourselves. Perhaps most importantly, it's about loving ourselves without limits. My children, in their innocence, mirrored this truth back to me, teaching me to extend that love inward and outward—to myself and the world.

I hope this book stirs doubts in you, the kind that ignites your own quest for meaning. May it guide you toward your unique path, where you uncover your own truths and perhaps catch a glimpse of unconditional love—for yourself and this wondrous, interconnected world we share.

How to Read This Book

Think of The Energy of You as the reflections of a once-doubtful, now-curious spiritual seeker. It's not a rulebook or a final answer to life's big questions. Instead, it's a tapestry of stories, insights, and tools that lit my way—offered here to spark your own discoveries. At the end, you'll find a "Take Action" section, a nod to my logical side and a gift for readers who, like the old me, crave something practical to do. But the heart of this book lies in the questions it raises, the seeds of curiosity it plants to guide you toward your own path.

If you read nothing else, I encourage you to start with the **first three and the last three chapters**. They hold the essence of my message and will give you a sense of what this book is really about. I've never read books in a straight line myself. I circle, skip, return, and linger where I feel called. I invite you to do the same. The message is what matters most.

The chapters in between introduce tools—Enneagram, Astrology, Human Design, Gene Keys, and others—that were signposts on my journey. They're not the only roads to truth, nor are they meant to be rigid doctrines. If a tool speaks to you, dive deeper; if not, simply move on. But if they resonate with you, I invite you to explore them further—dive into a book, join a workshop, or seek out your own teachers. But your journey is yours alone, and the answers you need are already around you, waiting for the right questions to unlock them.

Life, as I've come to see it, is a playful mystery—a game of synchronicities and hidden connections. The more you seek, the more you'll uncover. So, approach this book with an open mind, a light heart, and a willingness to doubt, question, and grow. Let it be a companion on your adventure, not the destination itself.

CHAPTER 1

THE MASK OF SURVIVAL

I've always considered myself to be a winner. I was born to win, I told myself. That's how life was set up for me. So, here's how the scene was set. I'm Nisha, the eldest daughter in a family with a rapidly growing business in India—sugar mills churning, liquor bottles clinking, hotels bustling, power plants humming, a sprawling empire. My dad came from nothing. He had no fancy degrees nor a powerful family name to lean on. But what he did have was a dream burning brightly in his chest. He was driven to build a better life for himself and for us, and he turned his grit into determination, crafting his success out of thin air. As a kid growing up in hot and humid Chennai, splashing through monsoon puddles, I knew deep down that I wanted a piece of that dream. Raised in a traditional South Indian family, I wasn't supposed to want it. In our culture, boys inherit the empires; they carry the torch. And girls? We're meant to build and nurture our families, stir pots, and nod along. But I wasn't buying into any of that.

I wrestled with being a girl from the very beginning. While my younger sister played with dolls, I chose toy guns and war games with my brothers. I did love the quiet wisdom being a girl gave me, though—a flicker of emotional maturity I felt even as I played ball with my brothers in the yard. Through the years as I grew into an adult, I simply couldn't stand the idea that my future simply would boil down to getting married and raising a family. Why should that be my ceiling? Increasingly, I wondered how I could take the reins of the business. I decided that building the skills required to run a business was what would pave my way. At 14, I started by shadowing Dad on school holidays—trailing him through our offices and factories, the air thick with the scent of ambition. It started small: that summer, I became the telephone operator for one of our smaller hotels. I remember those old phone exchanges like it was yesterday—those clunky beasts with cables you had to pull and plug to connect a call. The board would light up like a Christmas tree—red, green, blinking—and I'd sit there for hours, headset clamped on, voice steady, proudly repeating those words, "Connecting you now," like I was the world's gatekeeper. It wasn't much, just keeping the lines humming, but it made me feel like I was part of something—contributing to something larger than myself, even if it was just during the holidays. Strange thing was, in India back then, kids from affluent families didn't work, especially not girls. My siblings had the same shot—sitting in Dad's office, listening to the endless business chatter—but they thought it was pointless when they could be out doing kid stuff. My younger sister would rather braid her dolls' hair, and my brothers were off playing cricket. I didn't get it. I was hooked. Every meeting I attended widened my world, every barked order felt like a lesson to be learned.

Dad would mention my little role to his friends, proud as hell, and I'd puff up, thinking I'd done something special. "This is my daughter Nisha," he'd say, his voice glowing with warmth, "she's training at the hotel now." His friends—mostly bankers and bureaucrats he knew from work—would shoot me a smile and say, "So you are the clever one your dad's always on about." The pride in my father's voice always hit me in a powerful way, like fuel on a fire that was steadily burning. While my brothers and sister rolled their eyes, I was soaking it all in, loving that my world was expanding. But back then, I don't think anyone — not even Dad—really saw me as potentially taking the helm. In our conservative family, the script was set: girls dabble, help out, then move on to marriage and kids. Work was a phase, a mere sideshow before the real deal.

We lived in a large family home filled with cousins, aunts, and uncles—a "joint family." Heaven as a kid—all the playmates you could want, and the grown-ups barely noticed what you were up to. But at a different level, their scrutiny was a constant. When I was 16, an aunt visiting from our hometown in Kerala surveyed us, girl cousins, like market vegetables. "Soon they'll be running their own families," she said. I stared ahead in silence, but inside, I seethed. Why was that my finish line? Did Dad see me at the helm, or was I just his little shadow, a novelty to brag about? To get a sense of how rigid my family was, consider this: when I was a child, another aunt informed me, "In our culture, a 60-year-old woman should stand when a 6-year-old boy walks in." I remember thinking, well that's definitely bullshit. Every rule like that, every sidelong glance that said I wasn't enough, fueled me. I'd prove I was as good as any boy—better, even.

After that summer job at the hotel operating the phones, I continued going back every school break, shadowing my father, sitting in on meetings. As a teenager, the work started to become boring—and I struggled to keep up. Terms like "supply chains" and "profit margins" slipped right past me. I'd sit, chin on hand, feeling like a fraud, pretending I understood. But I didn't quit. Listening to them hash out deals was like trying to decipher code. They'd rant about bureaucratic hassles—licenses, regulations, the daily pressure to grease the wheels—and I'd sit there, lost. Business in India back then, especially in our tightly controlled industries, was a man's game. Red tape strangled everything, and the shady corners were just part of the deal. I'd watch Dad navigate all of it—calm, sharp, cutting through the constant demands like a knife—and I'd wonder, how does he do it? To my teenage mind, it was overwhelming, a tangle I couldn't unravel. How would I ever get this? Once, a smug bureaucrat stalled after taking his "gift.," As he sat there smirking, I could see Dad's angry response building. His voice stayed low, but his eyes were like steel: "Get this done." It seemed to me, he was "a superhero in a safari suit".

It seemed clear my father was quietly amused that his daughter showed so much interest in his business. He gave me my own table in a corner of his very large room that was dwarfed by his massive desk—and when there were discussions, he'd ask me to come and sit across his table with the visiting executives. They were probably particularly amused and surprised to see a teenage girl sitting in all the meetings, listening intently, trying to follow the business discussions and negotiations. I'd perch there, chin up, pretending I understood every word, even when half of it flew over my head.

I'd wait for Dad to come home when I returned from school, ears perked at attention, intent on catching his work stories over dinner. He'd lean back, recounting his experience of outsmarting a rival. "They thought they had me," he'd say with a grin, "but I don't bend." I lapped it up and began modeling his confidence. He loved to share his tales about work, detailing every challenge of his day with my mother as I listened quietly. I became enthralled listening to how he had managed to win a deal or outsmart a competitor. I could almost picture him walking away the winner as everyone around him looked on in awe. I loved all his stories—the highs and the lows, the wins and the losses. I came to recognize the look on his face as he weighed risks with a furrowed brow and his wins that were celebrated with a purposeful grin. I was lapping up every detail like a sponge, determined to learn it all. I studied him closely, modeling myself after his steady confidence and unshakeable drive. In undergrad, I spent more time at work. I picked a college option—mornings at the office with Dad, afternoons in class. I'd ride with him to work, settle in at my table, and watch him juggle calls, meetings, and paper stacks—barking orders, charming suppliers. I pretended to grasp the chaos. Some days, he'd ask for my input after a discussion and listen intently to what I said. That spark kept me going—I belonged, even if I didn't get the whole picture yet. By now, I had a better understanding of the business, but I was still mostly shadowing my Dad, studying him as I sat in on all the meetings

I could. There were times when, even I, wondered what I was getting out of it. But I was learning, and with every hour spent at the office, every scribbled note, I was delving deeper into the intricacies of our complex businesses. I was building my case, I was setting myself up to take over the business someday.

Then came the big leap—I decided to get an MBA from London Business School, a top-tier credential I knew my Dad couldn't brush off. This was still the day when daughters rarely took over the business. But as someone who did not have the opportunity to get a formal education, my father looked up to the people who had. I was convinced that he would see me as the real deal once I got my MBA. I could picture his nod of approval when I'd return with that degree in hand. But when I got accepted to London Business School—the only place to which I'd applied—because it had the most international class, perfect for running our business in a pre-globalization India—Dad shut it down. "No," he said, flatly. "You can go there after you're married. We'll find you a guy who wants an MBA too, and you can go together." I was devastated. After all the late nights, the grind, the application process, he couldn't let a single girl live alone in a foreign country? It stung like hell. I'd busted my ass to get in—top grades, killer essays, the works—and he was clipping my wings because of some outdated notion. Then Mom stepped up—she was the steady force. She was strict, and she had high standards on acceptable behaviour, especially for the girls in our family. Most times, she used the cane to keep us in line as kids. So when I was accepted into London Business School, I never expected her support. She fought for me, however, told Dad I'd earned it and that I deserved to go. It wasn't a loud or dramatic display, just her calm insistence chipping away at his will. "She's not like the others," she said one night over dinner, her voice soft but firm- "Let her try." She won. He acquiesced. I'll never forget that. My mom gave me wings when he'd tried to clip them. Now there was nothing stopping me from showing my Dad I was the one.

And he did see it. I returned to Chennai with my MBA tucked under my arm and, soon after, stepped into the CEO role for our flagship company, the beating heart of our empire. I had finally arrived. I felt sure I would have been happy to keep doing this for the rest of my life. I had been in a relationship before I joined the business. But I felt that I had to put that into a box along with everything else in the past so that I could move forward to this new chapter in my life—living my dream. Following the norm in my culture and to keep my parents smiling, I'd said yes to an arranged marriage—a nice guy, right family background—and soon I had two beautiful boys tumbling into my life. I was moving down my checklist, every box ticked with a flourish of pride. I'd made it, my boss-girl dreams pulsing through me, strutting through boardrooms with an unmistakable air of confidence. If you'd asked me then, "Nisha, what is the best version of you?" I'd have grinned widely and said, "Right here—leading, winning, being unstoppable." Life was golden, and it felt like the universe itself was cheering me on, every star twinkling in my favor.

Then 2006 rolled in like a thunderbolt out of nowhere and shattered my perfect life. My firstborn, my son, Arjun—almost 5 years old, a wise little soul with eyes that seemed to peer straight into my heart, who somehow always managed to keep me grounded—vanished in a week. A fever spiked overnight, turning our home into a haze of worry. The hospital swallowed us whole; white coats fluttering, machines beeping endlessly, a whirlwind of tests and by the end of that week, we were pulling the plug. I barely had time to register what had hit me, I was devastated, as any mother would be, but it was more than that. Shock sank into my bones, grief clawing at my chest, and I couldn't wrap my head around it—how could this happen to me? I'd always relied on hope and the raw strength of my determination to power through life, spinning every challenge into a win like some kind of magic trick. But this? Death was a wall I couldn't climb. No amount of grit or promises of a brighter tomorrow could bring Arjun back. I felt helpless; lost in a daze, numb and confused, caught in a surreal nightmare where I kept hoping I'd wake up and find him smiling at me at breakfast. But under my locked jaw and dry eyes, something else clawed at me. It was guilt, sharp and relentless. I'd been an absentee mother. My mom raised him more than I did. After he was born, I couldn't pause; less than a month and I was back at work, leaving him in her arms. I missed his first words, his first wobbly steps, brushing it off with the notion that I was building something bigger. Anyone can be a mother.

When Arjun was gone, that lie crumbled. The guilt weighed heavily on me even as it whispered, You weren't there, Nisha. In response, I pushed those thoughts deeper within, refusing to let them breathe. I knew that if I let them out, there would be a flood I couldn't dam up. I couldn't afford that—I was a survivor, a fighter. Pausing to feel it, drowning in remorse, would've made me weak. I couldn't let it happen.

And I didn't let it show. At the funeral, hundreds watched me—though it felt like thousands in my reeling mind—and I stood like a statue, silent, no wobble breaking through. The eyes around me softened with pity, and I hated how small it made me feel, like I'd failed the one test that mattered in life. So I dodged it all. I skipped the condolence visits lining up at our door and bolted to Singapore, to my safe space, with a shaky excuse about needing to recuperate. I had built my home in Singapore as a sanctuary when life in Chennai with my extended family had overwhelmed me. In time it had become my safe space—a sleek condo with floor-to-ceiling windows, the city skyline sprawling out like a vast promise. Back in Chennai, my friends would tiptoe around me, asking, "How are you?" and I'd swerve with a quick, "Oh, let's talk about something else," my voice brisk as a power-walk. I'd won folks over through the years —warm, fun Nisha once I opened up—but back then? I was stoic, snobbish, shut tight. I'd have spooked myself, too. I wasn't brave; I was blank.

How do you "fix" losing your kid? I decided powering through was the only way forward. I had another boy soon after—my son Rajiv, who was a balm for the ache that wouldn't quit—and dove right into work. My now eldest, Varun, who was three, was also perhaps experiencing trauma in his own way. He had lost his older brother and had no idea why all the grown-ups had changed overnight. He had always been attached to me, this clingy little shadow trailing me around the house, and maybe he needed his mother's reassurance at this time. I'd catch him staring at me, big eyes searching for something I couldn't give, and I'd turn away, muttering about a call I had to take. Turnarounds demanded my focus, and deals needed sealing. I had to prove to myself that I was still a winner and that my resolve could remain as solid as iron.

Meanwhile, my marriage started to fray. My husband, patient for too long, had found the attention he craved elsewhere and wanted out. We'd been wobbling from the start, holding it together for the kids with stiff smiles that didn't reach our eyes, and when it finally snapped after ten years, the split was messy. I felt the sting of betrayal and rejection when he moved away—his new life flashing in my face—but I brushed it aside. I was too busy surviving to let it sink in. "I don't need this," I told myself. "Work is my purpose; it's why I'm here." The family business needed me—for my kids, my legacy—and that focus kept me sane. I'd bury myself in what had to be done—meetings stacking up, numbers to crunch, wins to chase—and left no room for anything softer to creep in. Finally, I was getting settled into this groove, I thought to myself—I am back to my path.

But life, once again, had other plans for me. My Dad turned 80 and decided my two brothers should take a more active role in the business. He was being rational, acting like any traditional father would, wanting them woven into the fabric of it all, though he still saw me continuing at the helm. But I didn't take it that way. To me, it landed like a slap. My empire, my badge, the future I'd dreamed of running solo—they all seemed to fade before my eyes. Everything I'd dreamed up over the years—CEO, wife, mother—all my starring roles started to come apart, and suddenly my life felt like a sitcom without a punchline.

I didn't catch it back then, but I thought I'd mastered survival. Winners always survive! People would say, "You're so strong," and I'd nod in agreement, masking the chill that had settled deep inside me. Years later, I'd hug my boys—giggling, full of joy—and feel numb inside. My chest felt locked, my heart had turned to frost, emotions locked away. I desperately needed to dodge the painful sting of feeling that love had been stored away where I couldn't reach it. When my friends would share their struggles, divorces, setbacks, I was able to muster up some comforting words, but my heart stayed silent and cold, offering nothing at all—no empathy, no connection. My ex got a hollow version of me; honestly, it barely registered when he wanted out. After the initial pain, in fact, it was almost a relief. My kids deserved more than they got from me. I had tuned out everything—grief over Arjun, hurt from the marriage, fear of looking weak—and convinced myself that was my strength. Here's a little heads-up: it wasn't.

It was only much later that I would realize—all that I believed I was—maybe that's not the real me. And that mask I wore? I had created it when I was young. Growing up, I learned to hustle, to break past the norms stacked against me, to prove I was worth it. Dad's empire became my stage, and I was the star. Every deal was a spotlight, every win a cheer that solidified my sense of belonging. When life slammed into me—Arjun gone, my marriage crumbling—I fell back on that old script: don't feel, just keep doing. It wasn't only a mask; it became my identity—an achiever, a survivor, a winner. There's nothing wrong with wanting to win—I still do, and that's fine—but I'd let it define me completely, I thought that's all I was. It worked like a charm for a while—until it didn't. I'd sit amid Singapore's buzz or Chennai's heat, and to all appearances I was winning, but often I'd find myself wondering: Why is it so quiet in here? Empathy had vanished. I couldn't conjure it up even if I tried. I'd built a wall, brick by brick, shutting out the messiness of feeling anything real. People saw fun Nisha, wise Nisha—once I let them in—but inside me? It was cold as stale coffee.

Here's where it gets real: I didn't realize I'd lost myself along the way. I'd ask, "Who am I?" And the answer roared back: I'm the winner, the achiever, the survivor. I'd built this identity since I was a girl shadowing Dad, dreaming of steering empires, proving I'm not just the eldest daughter but the one who makes it happen. I'd marched through boardrooms, sealed deals, taken the CEO seat, fully convinced that's all I needed to be. Psychologists call it *overidentification*—when a role, like "girl boss" for me, swallows you whole; your thoughts orbit it endlessly, and anything less feels like failure. I'd tied my worth to that title, that drive—every pitch, every win feeding it—until life's jolts left me wondering if that's all there is. My story is not unique. It is just a variation of the countless stories in this world. And, surely, there are a vast range of experiences that are very intense. But who among us can claim to be an expert on the human experience? We can only share our perceptions that hopefully can help others on their journey.

We all wear masks—me with my achiever's crown, you with yours: the rock, the caretaker, the star. What role loops in your head, the one you can't let slip? That's where you might be over-identifying with your mask, behind which the real you hides. This was my tumble—and, next, we'll see what it cost me when that mask didn't hold fast. Fair warning: it's plenty. But beneath that role, something waited—the real me, itching to step out.

Take Action: Identify Your Mask and What It's Hiding

Grab a pen, and think of where in your life you push through, over-identifying with a role—like when I powered on with playing the unbreakable winner. What's one role that crowds your thoughts like my "winner" badge that I wore too tightly? Is it provider, perfectionist, protector, hero? Write it down: "I play the role of a…" Keep it simple, one line, no fuss.

Pause and say to yourself, "I'm more than this mask." Let it settle for a moment. Write one word that describes a positive attribute of yours that lies buried deep under this role—like "caring"—that hints at what's hiding beneath.

CHAPTER 2

THE NUMB YEARS – THE COLD COST

Life has a way of hurling curveballs just when you think you've mastered the game. I'd made it through that first major fall—my "winner" identity, forged in the blazing heat of my ambition, cracked under the burden of my expectations. Still, I pressed on, certain I had everything figured out. But as the years passed, a chill began to seep in, slow and sharp, numbing me in ways I never anticipated.

It struck me in my Chennai office, a place that once thrummed with my victories. Imagine this: I'm seated at my desk, papers scattered, the heartbeat of our empire—sugar mills, liquor brands, hotels, power plants—still echoing in my ears. My father, now 80, decides it's time to bring my brothers into the family business. He's not pushing me aside; he's just a father, weaving them into the story while I remain at the helm. But that's not how it feels. It's a sudden shock, a jolt that catches my breath, anger bubbling up like acid. For decades, I'd fought to prove myself—ignoring every whisper that girls can't lead, every doubting glance that questioned my right to be at the top. And now? My mind roars, "What, why am I not enough?"

Perception plays tricks, twisting reality into knots. When my brothers first joined, I didn't let it weigh on me too heavily. I was confident, and after all—I held all the cards. I knew the business inside and out, far better than they did. But my father saw his sons' potential too, and like any devoted parent, he was patient with them. He gave them room to grow, encouraged their ideas, even if it meant challenging some of my choices. To me, it felt like he was choosing sides. Take one case: my brother suggested a different way to handle a litigation, and I bristled at his approach. When my father opted to go with his plan, it stung deeply. That was just one instance, but as these incidents piled up, I became furious. I was becoming difficult to work with, guarding my strategies like a secret. After a couple of years, I was utterly discouraged, convinced my father wanted me to fade next to my brothers. I started to believe he'd built me up just to tear me down. It felt like my world was collapsing. Every day at the office became a battleground of aggression, and I was exhausted. That's when I told myself, "This is it."

In the past, I'd have stormed in, seizing full control with my bare hands. And at first, I tried—I went full survivor mode, raging against this perceived betrayal, determined to prove I was still the best, irreplaceable after everything I'd built. I fired off emails, dialed up contacts, clung to my authority in a game that now seemed rigged against me. But as the anger swelled, it unearthed shadows I'd buried long ago—hurt, betrayal, that relentless ache of being undervalued. These were emotions I'd only ever glimpsed before shoving them back into the darkness.

This time, they wouldn't quiet down. They overwhelmed me, a heavy sensation that I couldn't put a name to.

I felt isolated, like I was standing alone on an empty stage with no one left to hear my voice. A dark cloud rolled in—a depression I refused to acknowledge. I recall one morning, lying in bed, staring at the ceiling, thinking: Even if I didn't wake up today, who would really miss me? Maybe my boys, Varun and Rajiv, but they're young and tough—they'd carry on. The thought darted past, leaving a bitter aftertaste. I wanted to fight, to reignite that old flame, but it had been snuffed out by a weight I couldn't lift. Yet a faint spark lingered. I needed to win again, somewhere, somehow. Maybe not in our company; maybe that chapter was ending. So I pulled back, simmering with resolve, ready to forge my own path, to create something that shouted, "I'm still here." I'm a positive person at heart, fueled by a never-say-die spirit. I still believed I could succeed no matter the odds. I had the skills, the expertise, and the drive. I could launch a new business. But in my mind, it couldn't be small-scale—it had to be grand, something to prove my worth to everyone.

I dove into new projects, frantic to reclaim my ground, to show I was still the one who rises. In my Chennai office, steam rose from a coffee mug as I scribbled plans; in my Singapore home, I paced restlessly, ideas bursting forth like sparks. Sugar plants in Africa—I pictured endless fields swaying under the gentle Mara sun. An ed-tech startup for hotel management skills, reimagining lessons through technological advancements. A medication-dispensing business, rethinking pharmacies from the ground up. Each idea flared to life—emails flew out, a handshake hinted at "maybe," and that familiar thrill pulsed through me, victory glinting just ahead.

Then, nothing. Deals evaporated like mist, doors slammed shut before I could wedge them open, hope extinguished in an instant. It was as if life smirked, "Not this time, girl." I stared at crumpled notes from sleepless nights, whispering, "What's wrong with me?" I'd always had a knack for winning people over—sharp strategies, pitches that lit up rooms—but now? I knew my ideas were strong, airtight, yet they sank. Was I losing my edge? The rage dulled to a steady hum, and I pushed harder, stacking on more—more calls, more drafts, more dreams.

But nothing took hold. It felt like my life was on pause, the play button stuck no matter how I pressed it. I was accustomed to winning, to shaping the world to my will. Now, it was as if the universe murmured, "Sit still." And I didn't know how to do that.

Around this time, my divorce from my estranged husband was finalized. We'd been separated for years. Divorce is never easy, especially in India where marriage binds two families, not just two people. So we'd remained legally tied but apart for nearly a decade, living in separate cities, leading separate lives. My world was unraveling, and now I had to break the news to my young kids. Rajiv, at 10, didn't even realize things were off between his parents—it was the only dynamic he'd known. He assumed all families functioned this way: kids with the mother, father absent for long stretches. The divorce was swift, but my shame kept me silent. For ages, I didn't tell even my closest friends I was divorced. My family was in the dark, too; the truth trickled out slowly. To twist the knife, my ex-husband remarried and moved on relatively quickly, while I stood alone, stripped of everything I'd once cherished.

By then, I was furious with the entire world. I was a walking storm, lashing out at anyone or anything in my path. The boys learned to steer clear of me most days, wary of my temper. It wasn't until years later, with the wisdom time brings, that I realized how consuming my rage had been. I remember a telling moment; Rajiv was helping me fetch a large bin of papers from storage. His hand slipped, and it crashed to the floor with a loud thud. Normally, I'd have erupted, but this was a different "me". I just laughed, looked up, and said, "That's okay, I'll pick it up." Before I could move, I caught the sheer terror on Rajiv's face—he was petrified over dropping a stack of papers. That's how frightening I'd been to my 12-year-old.

With all that anger surging through me, my only refuge came in the evenings, when the day's wars at the office were over, and I retreated to my room, cocooned in solitude. That's when the numbing silently crept in. I was too cowardly to formally quit the business. Whenever I broached the subject with Dad, he'd hush me, insisting that as the eldest, it was my duty and responsibility to carry the family forward. My whole life had revolved around being dutiful—the good daughter, the eldest, never letting the family down, following every rule. I was fed up, but I still didn't officially step away. Instead, I grew indifferent. Calls about the business? I'd dodge them, letting apathy stack up like the unread emails in my inbox—I couldn't face the mess. Even without being there constantly, I could tell our company was stumbling. At first, I felt helpless, then resentful. Pre-Covid, I'd lose myself in

TV—late-night flashes of light, a jumble of sound I didn't follow, but it helped to muffle the silence that sliced too deep. I'd sit and stare, flipping channels without watching, or stand by the window, watching Chennai's bustle fade into darkness, telling myself it would sort itself out.

Then COVID hit, and the world ground to a halt. My new business plans stalled, too—no one wanted to talk deals anymore. Even with all my Chennai-Singapore trips, I'd never planned to settle in Singapore permanently. My boys had national service obligations that would take them to Singapore for a while, but I'd assumed I'd just visit, staying busy with the business in India. Now, everything had shifted. With no reason to remain in India while the boys were in Singapore, I took Varun, nearing 18, and Rajiv, 15—almost men now—and planted us there. No more back and forth, just us, locked in together. Time had slipped away. Varun was headed for Singapore's mandatory national service, Rajiv was growing tall and reserved, and I'd been too buried in my concerns to see it. Like many others, I sank into K-dramas—welcome marathons where I didn't have to think. No shame in it; it was universal. Me, who'd once scoffed at mindless shows, priding myself as the sharp elite—now I was hooked, diving into them late, letting my mind drift away.

And then, the family empire showed signs of stumbling. Regulatory tangles and missteps sliced off millions, a piece of our legacy lost. I wasn't in operations—hadn't been since Dad's changes—but it wounded me anyway. Those mills, those plants were my foundation, even from afar. Once, I'd have leaped in, shoulders squared, trying to fix everything. This time, I felt held back by a force I couldn't identify. In a quiet corner of my mind, I felt relieved by the thought that this could be someone else's problem.

But it was more than relief—it was a blow that hit hard. In India, business isn't just money; it's your identity, your stamp on the world. When it crumbles, it's not just a financial loss—it's a public disgrace, a mark that shouts "failure." For me, defined by the empire I'd helped build, it was devastating. I felt it in the increasingly quiet days that passed—fewer emails, fewer calls about the business. Even at just a board level, there'd been plenty to keep me occupied, but now it was just lawsuits and headaches I didn't want to touch, along with my refusal to attend events because I had felt I'd come up short, leading to my avoidance of old colleagues. It was like I'd faded in the world's eyes, and certainly in my own. I wanted to be the brilliant businesswoman, the pioneer who could beat the odds. Now, my scorecard screamed "failed," and the voices persisted in my head: "She couldn't hold it together." "Maybe she wasn't good enough."

The shame became a burden I hauled around, and the questions were on a relentless loop in my head.What went wrong? Why wasn't I enough? I replayed every decision, every word, searching for where I'd slipped. But no answers emerged, only my doubts echoed back. In Singapore, removed from the chaos, it was somewhat easier to act like it wasn't my load to carry. The distance softened the pain—no one expected me to fix it—and I told myself I was free of it all, as if it were a task I'd never wanted. But it was deeper—I was evading the judgment, the evidence of my shortcomings, the fear that I wasn't as clever as I'd believed.

Life quieted to a whisper, leaving me with just myself, Varun, and Rajiv. They talked and laughed, filling the otherwise-silent house—I'd numbed myself with TV for years, saying, "Mummy needs her me time." Now, I could no longer hide by numbing and I didn't want to. I started cooking—me, who'd rejected kitchens because Dad commanded empires, not stovetops. I'd battled the traditional female role since childhood, but here I was, stirring pots, surprised by the feeling of warmth I felt as I set plates down, bonding with my boys over my home-cooked meals. It was late, but it was genuine.

Singapore had always been my retreat, a place to recharge, but I'd kept to myself, no ties beyond my bubble. Now, I craved more. I built a circle—starting with Mahjong sessions with women who were mostly expats, though some were local. I'd never had many female friends, not truly. I couldn't connect to their chatter, especially the homemakers, with my mind always on business. But this was new. Afternoons filled with tiles clicking, food passing around and laughter flowing freely. It was effortless, this connection—women sharing tales, viewpoints I'd never stopped to consider. Covid's rules kept groups tight, and the closeness grew. We took long walks through Singapore's nature parks, greenery I'd forgotten I adored. It wasn't just the walking that nourished me—it was the conversations, raw and rich, unveiling lives I'd never pictured. I felt connected and seen in a fresh light.

I half heartedly tested my business ideas again—phone calls, quick chats—but my heart was elsewhere, in Mahjong, walks, cooking for my boys. I wondered if this was avoidance. Am I going soft, and that's why nothing's working? The self-doubt gnawed at me as I drifted to sleep, so I smothered them with K-dramas. No thinking, just subtitles to follow—a blankness I needed.

Time blurred, and I was just cooking, joking with Varun and Rajiv, connecting with my women's group. It was a simple kind of happiness. The sun stayed hidden, but the air felt warmer. Something was stirring in me, though I didn't notice it then. Pre-COVID, after my brothers joined the business, I'd dabbled in spiritual retreats and wellness programs to calm my restless mind. They'd come randomly—friends prodding me when work waned—so I went: a wellness resort in Thailand, a yoga retreat in India, the Hoffman Process in Australia. I was still guarded, but something slipped through, easing a discomfort I couldn't name. Covid's pervasive stillness amplified it. I was present, truly present, seeing my boys, not just skimming by. I hugged them and laughed heartily with them for the first time in a long time. My chest wasn't iced over anymore.

I even started playing the piano. It was fresh, unconnected to business or proving myself—just for me. The notes faltered at first, but there was calmness that prevailed, a quiet delight in growth that didn't require outside recognition. It was subtle, and I began to realize that not everything has to be a conquest.

I'd sit with Varun, planning his future, watch Rajiv buried in a book, and win over my new friends once I let them in. But inside, there was a feeling I couldn't mute, no matter how many K-dramas I binged or how casually I tried to dismiss it. The fury at the changes, the business falling apart, the dread of fading into oblivion.The idea of facing it all was still too raw. Life hit me hard, and I froze it out. It takes a toll.

What was worse: I didn't recognize how much I'd dulled my feelings. Yet I'd encounter only a void where life should thrum. I'd kept moving—new projects, dodging tangles—but feeling? Vanished. Numbing myself with distractions could only do so much. Deep down there was still anger at the unwelcome changes in my life. There was also the fear of losing it all. I had muffled it all because sitting with it hurt too much. Yet, life kept hammering away, trying to jolt me awake. You've got your ways of escaping too—computer time, television screen, drinking, grinding. How do you numb your feelings?

Take Action: Name Your Avoidance

Grab a pen, recall a rough patch—like when I sank into K-dramas to dodge the silence after the business started to plummet. How did you dodge the tough stuff? Write it down: "I dodged challenges by…" One line, unedited, is fine. Read what you've written, take a moment to pause, and sit with it for a while." Let your awareness settle. What slipped out when you didn't try to avoid your feelings—like my rage at my family, or the sense of dread I wouldn't admit? Then boil it down to one word—like "fear." That's what you're avoiding. Try not to look away. The power of your clear perspective is freeing, so open up to the possibility that you can be with your feelings, without being consumed by them. What we run from, follows us.

CHAPTER 3

AWAKENING – THE STIRRINGS OF ENERGY

For too long, the joy in my life had been muted. I had grown used to a droning grayscale existence where days bled into one another, each as unremarkable as the last. I'd retreated into routine, constructing a fortress of predictability to shield myself from the possibility of chaos I couldn't confront. That was Chapter 2: a numbing cocoon I hadn't even noticed I'd spun around myself until something began to break through. It wasn't a grand, cinematic moment—no bolts of lightning splitting the sky, no angelic choirs heralding change—just a faint stirring, a soft whisper, persistent and undeniable. This is Chapter 3—awakening, the stirrings of energy. It slipped into my life quietly, reshaping me one breath, one tear, one heartbeat at a time.

A Reluctant Seed: The Echo of Raja Yoga

It all began with a book, "Raja Yoga," by Swami Vivekananda, a text I stumbled upon almost by chance. I wasn't seeking spirituality—least of all from Hinduism, a tradition I'd turned my back on since childhood. Growing up Indian, I'd viewed it as an elaborate labyrinth of rituals that was restrictive and, too often, dismissive of women—demanding a blind faith I couldn't summon. Yoga, in my mind, was just another circuitous path—slow, pointless, and drenched in dogma. But Raja Yoga defied my expectations. Vivekananda peeled back the ceremonial veneer and offered something starkly practical: control your mind, test everything through your own experience, and uncover the divine within yourself. It wasn't about distant gods; it was about self-mastery, a logic that sparked my curiosity even as I resisted it.

The book had been languishing on my shelf, buried under a layer of dust for months, a silent relic of a fleeting impulse purchase. At that point in my life, I had rejected Hinduism, convinced it had nothing to offer but outdated traditions and empty gestures. In turning away, though, I hadn't realized I was also discarding a vast reservoir of ancient wisdom—wisdom I'd unknowingly been searching for all along. It wasn't the essence I had been wary of; it was the packaging—the ornate rituals, the rigid expectations—that had pushed me away. Then Raja Yoga entered the frame, and with it, everything shifted.

This wasn't just another spiritual tome gathering dust; it was Vivekananda's incisive take on Patanjali's Yoga Sutras, an ancient manual for taming the mind and revealing the divine spark within. I'd braced myself for more dogma, more rules, but what I uncovered was a roadmap that was practical and tangible. It stripped away the rituals I'd grown to resent and laid bare Hinduism's beating heart: a science of the self, as potent today as it was millennia ago. Here's how it turned my perspective upside down and nudged me onto a spiritual path I had never imagined I'd tread.

A New Lens on Hinduism

As a child, I'd seen Hinduism through a haze of ceremonies—intricate, exclusionary, and often relegating women to the margins. It clashed with my hunger for meaning, leaving me frustrated and disconnected. But Raja Yoga, as defined by Vivekananda, rewrote that narrative. Vivekananda framed yoga not as a series of physical contortions (though those have their place), but as a disciplined method to master your inner world. He distilled the ancient teachings of Patanjali, which hold that every soul is inherently divine, into a bold challenge. Vivekananda stated that each individual can realize that divinity by gaining command over the external chaos and the restless mind. Rituals? Dogmas? Temples? They're peripheral, he explained. The true work unfolds within. Vivekananda explained that wisdom springs from experience—that religion is merely a set of beliefs until you live it—and that the practice of yoga equips you with the tools to turn your mind into a clear window to your inner universe.

That really struck me. I'd been so consumed with rejecting Hinduism's rituals that I'd overlooked its profound depths. Raja Yoga revealed a practical philosophy that was also a toolkit for living with intention and serenity. It wasn't about appeasing celestial overseers; it was about claiming my own power. In that moment of realization, Hinduism had transformed into a source of strength, a wellspring of empowerment I hadn't anticipated.

The Eight Limbs: A Practical Path

At the core of Raja Yoga are the eight limbs of yoga, a step-by-step journey from ethical foundations to transcendent self-realization. It begins with Yama and Niyama—guidelines like non-violence, truthfulness, and contentment. These weren't lofty platitudes; they were concrete habits I could cultivate, small behavioral shifts in how I interacted with the world, concrete habits I could cultivate. Next came Asanas (postures) and Pranayama (breath control), which I approached with a mix of skepticism and intrigue. Sitting tall, breathing consciously and purposefully—it seemed almost too basic to be effective. Yet these practices anchored me in a way I hadn't felt before, tethering my scattered thoughts to the present moment.

The later limbs—Pratyahara (withdrawing the senses), Dharana (concentration), Dhyana (meditation), and Samadhi (super-consciousness)—loomed like distant peaks, intimidating and out of reach. But Vivekananda made them approachable by illuminating their purpose. The mind, he said, is a wild horse, bucking and bolting through life's turmoil if left unrestrained. With practice, you can bridle it, and that's where the transformation begins. I dipped my toe in, starting with meditation—just sitting still—five minutes a day, then stretching to ten. Slowly, a stillness began to bloom within me, unfamiliar and quiet, gently dissolving the bitterness I'd harbored toward Hinduism as I witnessed its wisdom unfold in real time.

Reading "Raja Yoga" felt like drawing back a heavy curtain and flooding a dim room with light. I'd been so fixated on dismissing the rituals that I'd missed the pragmatism they concealed.

Vivekananda's mantra—"Believe nothing until you find it out for yourself"—echoed in my bones. I began to realize that I didn't have to swallow Hinduism whole; I could experiment with it. So I did. I sat in silence, I reflected, I tried to root myself in the moment. And gradually, I felt lighter, my mind sharper, my heart less burdened.

The book also reshaped my perception of women in Hinduism. I'd long felt that the tradition pushed us aside, but Raja Yoga transcended those limitations. Its practice is agnostic to gender or rank—it's for anyone who is ready to embrace it. The divine sense of self isn't a privilege doled out to the chosen; it's a birthright we all carry. That insight dispelled my resentment, replacing it with a sense of wonder. What else had I misjudged?

Why It Matters Today

What floored me most about Raja Yoga was its timeless nature. Swami Vivekananda's *Raja Yoga*, penned over a century ago, feels tailor-made for our frenetic, modern lives. Vivekananda speaks of harnessing Prana—the vital life force coursing through all things—and channeling it to master mind and body. This isn't airy mysticism; it's a hands-on discipline, applicable whether you're gridlocked in traffic or grappling with self-doubt. I began weaving its lessons into my days—breathing through tension, steadying my focus when my thoughts spiraled—and it delivered.

For me, the study and practice of Raja Yoga brought me to a crucial pivot point. It didn't simply alter my view of Hinduism; it rewired how I viewed myself. I'd been adrift, yearning for an anchor to moor my spiritual quest, and this book handed me the raw materials to forge one. It's not about escaping the world—it's about a new way of being with it, one deliberate breath, one focused thought at a time. Hinduism, I came to see, isn't the obstacle; it's a lens we can peer through. Wipe away the excess, and what remains is wisdom—practical, profound, and undeniably human.

I was drawn to its clarity, its no-nonsense approach—no incense-clouded mysticism, but a practical methodology. Yet due to the way in which I was raised, I instinctively recoiled from Hinduism, yoga, and all the gurus I'd written off as background noise. Still, a quiet part of me bowed to the wisdom—somewhat grudgingly, almost secretly—and though I didn't embrace it outright, it planted itself like a seed, giving rise to the question: What if there's more?

A Stirring Breeze: Thailand's Unexpected Gift

That seed swelled into bloom during a trip to Thailand, a spontaneous detour to a health resort I'd chosen for its functional medicine, not its spiritual trappings. I'd gone to recharge my body—worn thin from plotting my next steps after a rift with my father and brothers. I had been teetering on the edge of a meltdown from the stress, but I knew I needed a digital detox, to be stripped of my phone's constant buzz. The February air hung warm and gentle, kissed with the zest of lemongrass and lime from meals that jolted my dulled senses awake. With hours to fill, I skimmed through the list of the resort's offerings and paused at "Chakra Balancing," led by a Japanese woman. I smirked—me, the original Indian cynic who'd jettisoned all that "woo-woo" fluff, signing up for what I assumed would be a fancy nap. Why not? I shrugged. At worst, I'd catch up on some sleep.

The room I entered was a quiet sanctuary, fragrant with citrus and sandalwood. I stretched out on a mat, arms limp at my sides, anticipating nothing more than restfulness. She didn't lay a hand on me but swept her open palms through the air above—and then I felt a surge, like a sudden gust of wind from my scalp down to my toes and swirling around my chest. There were no gadgets, and this was no sleight of hand. I felt an unmistakable hum thrumming through my bones. I chuckled with surprise under my breath and tried to dismiss it as a quirk, a one-off. Despite my initial skepticism, that electric feeling clung to me, a persistent vibration that was coaxing me nearer to the light. Something was awakening, and no attempts at brushing it off could erase its imprint.

The Crack Widens: Breathwork in South India

That fissure from the chakra balancing, yawned even wider at a spiritual workshop in South India, a four-day retreat that a friend had invited me to attend. I went dragging my feet, cynicism in tow, after decades of scoffing at these seemingly sanctimonious practices. This workshop dangled the promise of transformation through breathwork, guided by a guru whose thick accent and overtly tranquil persona rubbed me the wrong way. Holy men tended to raise my hackles—but I stayed, thanks to a mix of curiosity and a stubborn urge to debunk it all. The days seemed long— hours of listening to the guru's droning voice, steering us through countless rounds of deep breathing while I sat cross-legged, with my legs aching in silent protest.

The retreat was a grind. We rose before dawn, the air thick with humidity and the scent of incense, confined to a stark hall with bare walls and unforgiving floors. The guru droned on about surrender, energy, and syncing body with mind, but I mostly tuned him out, zeroing in on the breathwork instead. It kicked off simply: deep inhales through the nose, measured exhales, a rhythm that felt awkward at first. My mind churned—the recent argument with my Dad had left me raw, and my plans for the future were faltering—but as the breathing practice continued, something gave way. The breaths grew deeper, fiercer, almost feral. My chest swelled, my hands steadied, and then it rose: a pillar of calm, climbing from my gut to my head, warm and soothing. This wasn't mere relaxation—it was vibrant energy, and it felt as if my body had become rooted to a lifeline amid the chaotic thoughts that tried to intrude.

The teacher urged us to keep up with the practice after returning home from the retreat, so I did—for 21 days straight, driven by sheer mule-headed resolve. Once back in Chennai, I doubled down. Every morning, I'd perch on the hardwood floor of my home, eyes closed, tracing the sequence we'd drilled through: a cycle of inhales and exhales, shifting in force and pace. The first week was a slog—my thoughts buzzed like gnats, my legs seized up—but by day seven, it all snapped into place. A profound stillness took hold, not the deadened haze I'd once mistaken for peace, but a living, breathing calm. Each session sloughed off a layer of strain I hadn't known I was carrying. My anger dulled, my agitation hushed. I didn't morph into a disciple—still too quick with a quip to go all-in on the spiritual bit—but I had emerged from that workshop altered. The stress of my life—business hiccups, family spats—didn't dissolve, but its claws lost their hold. I could observe it all without being dragged under, and for the first time, I felt a spark of hunger for this newfound clarity. "This is real," I thought, the calm lingering like a welcome guest who'd settled in. It raised a question in my searching mind: What is this energy, and where is it pulling me?

After a month, I let the practice drop. Maybe the skeptic in me prevailed, or maybe I balked at leaning too hard into something I couldn't pin down. But the effects didn't vanish. That sense of calm morphed into a steady companion, sanding down the jagged edges of my days. Life's upheavals still rolled in—emails stacked up, calling for my attention, tempers flared in the family—but none of it dismantled me. The breathwork had cracked open a window to something deeper, a stability I hadn't known I could access.

I later learned that the practice I had learned at the workshop riffed on ancient yoga, distilled into a 21-minute ritual of breath and meditation—a shortcut for the casual seeker. The guru behind it still didn't win me over—my wariness of spiritual types ran too deep—but the method itself was ironclad. Each breath wove a thread, knitting my frayed edges back together. It wasn't about the teacher; it was about the shift inside me. The workshop had pried me apart, and the breathwork flooded the gaps with light.

The Flood Breaks: The Hoffman Process

Those whispers of a new approach to life were amplified at the Hoffman Process, an eight-day crucible that smashed through my remaining walls like a tempest. Once again, I had enrolled halfheartedly, griping about the expense and the time—but I was pulled by a growing desire to discover what else I had missed. The process vowed to unravel the knots we carry from childhood, fusing intellect, emotion, body, and spirit into what they dubbed the "quadrinity." I walked in with my guard up, but in spite of myself, I experienced a tidal shift in the days ahead. I didn't clock it until it engulfed me.

The days were merciless. We yelled, we breathed, we scribbled in our journals until our wrists throbbed. One afternoon, mid-session, a rush of feelings erupted in my chest; it was a torrent, scalding and untamed. Tears streaked my face, then laughter tore through, my voice splintering as I spoke truths I'd entombed for decades. It was messy—snotty, chaotic, unpolished—but when the storm passed, a peacefulness sank in more deeply than anything I'd touched before.

I think it was there, in the Hoffman Process, that I finally gained access to the immense grief I had been holding down since the loss of Arjun. It was as if I let myself unlock the vault, allowing every memory to surface—first the raw and jagged ones, then the waves of love and laughter. That, I believe, is what pried my heart wide open. The me who'd become emotionally deadened and barricaded from empathy, felt a crack in that wall. And here's how it unfolded: on the final day, sitting next to a stranger—a woman I'd barely exchanged words with—a warmth blossomed between us, a love so tangible it jolted me. Empathy, lost to me for years, surged back—raw, unguarded, alive. I left vibrating, and the energy coursing through me was now a full-throated roar.

The Hoffman Process shoved my childhood in my face. I'd grown up shadowing my father—his gait, his ambition, his relentless need to prove himself. As an Indian daughter, the pressure hit me twice as hard. It was an unceasing cycle of striving and performing. This molded me into someone who coped by shutting out my feelings—numbing out with TV, brushing off my sons Varun and Rajiv with aloofness. The process stripped it all bare: visions of my younger self, unsent letters to my parents, screams muffled into pillows that reverberated with decades of buried sorrow. Each task in the process chipped at my armor, exposing the girl beneath—frightened, hopeful, worthy without the need to earn it.

One scene burned into me. They asked us to picture our parents as kids, to see their scars, their own shaping. I saw my father—not as the rigid man I knew, but a boy, hesitant yet reaching out to be seen. The fury I'd harbored softened into comprehension, then forgiveness. The deluge that followed wasn't just catharsis; it was liberation. I saw how my father's habits had bled into mine, how I'd unwittingly cast shadows onto my sons. The process didn't wipe them away—it armed me with the tools I needed to release the shadows, to step into a lighter self.

That bond I shared with the stranger on the last day cemented it. We'd bared our stories, our wounds, and with that exposure, my defenses crumbled. I felt her like she was my kin—and not just her, but myself, my sons, and the world itself. Empathy, long dormant, roared awake. The Hoffman Process didn't just expose my patterns; it rewrote them, leaving me tender, open, and fiercely alive.

The Energy Roots Deep

The welcome changes I had experienced at the workshop didn't ebb when I returned home—they continued to flow. I'd sit by my window, city lights winking below, memory of Thailand's buzz echoing through me. After the workshop, I'd pad across my apartment, bare feet on cool marble, that calm pillar of peace steadied me as I contemplated life's big questions. Post-Hoffman, the sense of peacefulness grew stronger. Many nights, I'd awaken with tingling palms, a pervasive calmness threading through my breath. In my daily life, it seeped into the mundane as unexpected moments of joy: the soft glow of dawn through my window, the warmth of sunlight on my hands, a quiet smile shared in passing. I'd been like a machine—detached, mechanical—but now I was alive, gloriously messy and wide awake.

That revitalizing energy was exciting, and it made me more curious about the potential for further inner exploration. It began with Raja Yoga's seeds of wisdom, stirred by Thailand's breezes and sprouted in the practice of conscious breathing. The blossoming of growth culminated in an awakening brought on by the Hoffman Process. Late one night, notebook splayed, I scrawled: What if I let this mysterious process guide me? What if it's real, even if I can't label it? I filled pages with doubt, hope, and streaks of possibility. It wasn't about hard evidence; it was about a truth I felt, however difficult to convey in words.

My path to awakening wasn't a straight line. Some days, the old numbness crept back, heavy and familiar and I felt as if I was slogging through. But the energy always rallied, fiercer with each return. I'd feel that breeze, sense that pillar of calmness within me—a testament to what defies explanation yet persists. One night, standing in my kitchen, the city sprawling beyond the glass, I grasped it more completely. Raja Yoga had hinted, Thailand had teased, the yoga workshop had nurtured, and Hoffman had unleashed more lasting change. Yet there was something more calling to me at a vibratory level, and that energy was alive in my hands.

Take Action: Stir Your Own Energy

Awakening doesn't demand a spotlight or a pilgrimage—it starts right where you are. You don't need a guru or a retreat; you just need to experience it for yourself. Here's how to kindle your own stirrings of energy and invite the possibility of something more:

Pause and Reflect: Carve out five quiet minutes—by a window, on a stroll. What's one thing you've shoved aside that keeps resurfacing? Jot it down. Let it sit.

Feel the Breeze: Stand still, eyes closed, and picture a rush of air sweeping through you—head to toes. Breathe into it for a minute. What feelings does it stir within you? Scribble it, even if it's just "weird."

Breathe Deeply: Sit easy, inhale through your nose for four counts, hold for four, exhale for six. Do this five times. Where do you feel the calm or the spark? Take note.

Ask "What If?": Before bed, write one question: "What if there's more for me?" No answers—just let it hang in the air. See what drifts up by morning. Write it down.

Start small—positive energy thrives wherever you make room for it.

CHAPTER 4

THE PAUSE – CRACKING THE SHELL

Life has a way of shaking you to your core when it's time for change, and for me, that seismic shift hit with COVID. I found myself stranded in Singapore with my boys, the familiar rhythm of my Chennai commute fading into a distant memory. Then the family business—our legacy, my anchor—imploded. Regulations tightened like a noose, decisions backfired spectacularly, and millions evaporated into thin air. A massive piece of my roots, my very identity, slipped out of my grasp. Instead of trying to fight for what I thought I was losing, I threw myself into the hustle of new deals, new ventures, anything to keep moving. But nothing clicked, nothing stuck. Yet something had shifted inside me after diving into yoga and absorbing the new knowledge that had crept into my life over the past months. I was starting to see the world through a different lens, though I couldn't quite name it yet. Life was pressing down hard, relentless, and most days, I had my moments of calm. But I was also still pushing back with equal force—until another random workshop came along and cracked me wide open.

This book isn't about drifting off into some ethereal, spiritual fantasy land where logic doesn't apply. It's about taking the esoteric—the mysterious, the abstract—and making it practical, something I can wrap my hands around and wrestle with my mind. I've got a logical brain—sharp, skeptical, always questioning—and I was not willing to abandon it for vague, fuzzy emotions. Our minds are tools, precision instruments designed to guide us toward purpose, to help us unravel the big question: Why are we here? But purpose doesn't just appear like a gift-wrapped package unless you know who you are—not the polished, world-approved version of you, but the raw, unfiltered truth beneath the surface. We're all piled high with layers of conditioning—family expectations, societal norms, decades of playing roles we didn't audition for—that smother our authentic selves. The Hoffman Process taught me that. But peeling back those layers takes courage, persistence, and a starting point. For me, that anchor was the Enneagram, a system that maps out nine distinct personality types, each driven by its own unique motivations, fears, and quirks. It's not some mystical fluff; it's a structured framework my analytical mind can dig into, a first real swing at stripping away the mask I'd worn for years.

The Workshop: A Collision of Chance and Clarity

The Enneagram workshop didn't waltz into my life with a polite introduction—I stumbled over it by accident. A friend called me out of the blue, asking if I could take her spot at a workshop because she couldn't make it at the last minute. I said yes and slid into her place, stepping into a meeting room with stark white walls that felt cold and clinical. Everyone there seemed to know each other, chatting easily, while I stood apart, knowing only one friend in the crowd. Skepticism took hold of me—was this going to be one of those touchy-feely workshops where I'd be expected to spill my guts to strangers? I'd already been through that with the Hoffman Process, a deep emotional dive a while back, and I wasn't sure I was ready to go there again. So I started off guarded, silent, arms crossed, mentally preparing myself for what I wanted to get out of this experience.

For months, I'd been wrestling with questions about what I wanted to do with my life. The pace had slowed since COVID hit—days filled with Mahjong games, nature walks, cooking for my boys, and quiet time with friends—and I wondered if I'd outgrown the business world entirely. Did it even interest me anymore? Where was that old fire, that aggressive, can-do spirit that used to drive me? It felt like life had lulled me into a strange, artificial complacency, a facade I wasn't sure I could trust. Was I fooling myself? I couldn't wrap my head around the idea of stepping away from business completely—it had defined me for so long. Maybe there was a different way to approach it, a new path I was meant to take. All the buzz about purpose and impact kept swirling in my mind; maybe that was what I needed to explore. So when I saw the workshop flyer with that one bold line—"Do you want to find your life purpose?"—it had hooked me. I tried googling the workshop and the facilitator, hunting for details online, but came up empty. No website, no reviews, nothing. Still, I told myself that at least I knew the questions I wanted answered. That was enough to get me through the door.

I walked in claiming Type 8, the Challenger—CEO Nisha, tough as nails, always coming out on top. I'd taken Enneagram tests online multiple times before, and every result pointed to 8. I loved that label: self-confident, strong, assertive, a natural leader. It fit the image I had formed for myself perfectly. But on day one, the facilitator—a guy with a calm, grounded vibe and an unnervingly steady gaze—looked me over and dropped a little bomb on me. "You're a 2 - Helper," he said, casually, as if he were commenting on the weather. It hit me like a slap. Who's this guy to tell me who I am? I dove into the Type 2 description, and it was everything my hard-edged Type 8 shell rejected: nurturing, giving, connecting, all about relationships. That wasn't me—I wasn't some soft-hearted carer. I barely felt emotions most days, or so I told myself. I'd been so sure of my 8 identity, reveling in its power and independence. But this facilitator had a different way of uncovering our types, and it threw me off balance.

His approach didn't consist of the usual checklist of a hundred questions I'd answered online—questions where cognitive bias could easily sneak in and skew the results. Instead, he started with what he called the emotional lens: Are you an anger, shame, or fear type? What's the first emotion that surges up when life comes at you hard? Most people, he said, have a gut-level awareness of their primary emotional reaction. If that didn't clarify things, he moved to the center lens: Are you a head, heart, or gut type? Then came the style lens: Do you approach life with competency, outlook, or intensity? This reflective process felt raw, unfiltered, forcing me to look inward in a way that those quick quizzes never had. I was convinced there was no way I was a Type 2. When I read the description—empathetic, sincere, warm-hearted, friendly, generous, self-sacrificing, but also sentimental, flattering, and people-pleasing—I was triggered. It felt like an insult to the fierce, no-nonsense winner I'd always been.

The Enneagram doesn't stop at your core type; it refines it with "wings"—the numbers on either side of your type that add flavour to your personality. The theory is that one of the two wings is stronger, shaping how your core type shows up in the world. For me, they suggested a 3 wing, making me a potential 2w3. That sounded marginally better than a straight-up 2, but when I read the 2w3 description—nurturing mixed with ambition and a drive for success—I still bristled. It was more palatable than the 2w1, the idealistic, principled version of a Helper, but it didn't erase my resistance. I'd buried any hint of softness so deep, toughened up to embody the Type 8 I thought I had to be. This challenge to my "winner Nisha" identity shook me to the core. I wanted to bolt, and it had me muttering, "I'm no sidekick," but I stayed, teetering on the edge. Something clicked, though—a buried part of me, a giving self that had been smothered under years of grit, was now finding its way out. It was uncomfortable, but there was a flicker of relief, like rediscovering a piece of myself I'd lost long ago.

What Is the Enneagram?

To understand this upheaval, let's break down the Enneagram itself. It's a personality-typing system with roots stretching back centuries, blending ancient wisdom with modern psychology. Some trace its origins to early Christian mystics or Sufi traditions, but it was formalized in the 20th century by figures like George Gurdjieff and later Oscar Ichazo and Claudio Naranjo. The Enneagram maps nine core personality types, each defined by a central motivation, a basic fear, and a unique way of seeing the world. It's not just a label; it's a tool for self-awareness and growth, showing how we operate at our best and worst—and how we can evolve. Here's a rundown of the nine types:

1. **The Reformer** - Principled, purposeful, self-disciplined, perfectionistic. Driven by a need to be good and right.
2. **The Helper** - Generous, caring, people-pleasing, possessive. Motivated by a need to be loved and needed.
3. **The Achiever** - Adaptable, ambitious, driven, image-conscious. Fueled by a desire to succeed and be valued.
4. **The Individualist** - Expressive, creative, self-absorbed, moody. Seeking identity and authenticity.
5. **The Investigator** - Perceptive, analytical, secretive, detached. Driven by a need for knowledge and security.
6. **The Loyalist** - Responsible, loyal, anxious, cautious. Motivated by a need for safety and support.
7. **The Enthusiast** - Spontaneous, optimistic, scattered, thrill-seeking. Chasing freedom and happiness.
8. **The Challenger** - Bold, assertive, confrontational, protective. Driven by a need for control and strength.
9. **The Peacemaker** - Calm, agreeable, complacent, conflict-avoidant. Seeking peace and harmony.

Each type has wings—adjacent numbers that blend into the core personality. A Type 2 with a 3 wing (2w3) might be warm and giving but also ambitious and polished, while a 2w1 leans toward idealism and moral clarity. The system also groups types into triads based on their dominant energy centers—gut (8, 9, 1), heart (2, 3, 4), and head (5, 6, 7)—and their primary emotional drivers: anger, shame, or fear. This workshop's method layered these lenses—emotion, center, and style—to peel back surface behaviours and reveal the deeper truth. For me, it suggested a shift from the anger-driven, gut-centred, intense Type 8 to the shame-fueled, heart-based, outlook-focused Type 2. Everything about that felt wrong—until it didn't.

A Broader Dive: Beyond the Enneagram

The workshop didn't stop at the Enneagram—it was a full immersion into the chaotic, beautiful mess of being human, exploring a slew of concepts that all pointed to one truth: everything is energy—and the quality of that energy and our relationship with it determines the nature of our experience. Let's unpack each one and see how they reshaped my perspective.

The Six Human Needs

First up was the six human needs, a framework from Tony Robbins, a well-known life coach and motivational speaker. He argues that all human behaviour is driven by six universal needs:

Certainty - The need for safety, stability, and predictability in life.

Uncertainty/Variety - The craving for change, excitement, and new experiences.

Significance - The desire to feel important, unique, and valued by others.

Connection/Love - The need for intimacy, belonging, and emotional bonds.

Growth - The drive to learn, develop, and expand one's potential.

Contribution - The urge to give back, help others, and make a difference.

Everyone has all six, but we prioritize them differently based on our personality and experience. The twist? How we meet these needs can be constructive (building healthy habits), neutral (harmless routines), or destructive (unhealthy coping mechanisms). For me, significance and certainty had ruled my world—being the best, staying in control, always winning. Connection and growth were also important to me, but contribution barely registered on my radar. I'd chased significance through business victories and certainty through relentless planning. That craving for significance turned destructive, leaving me restless, pacing, and unmoored. The workshop showed me that these needs are energy in motion—when channeled well, they fuel us; when blocked or misdirected, they drain us.

The Iceberg Analogy

Next came the iceberg analogy, a classic in psychology that struck me deeply this time around. Picture an iceberg: the tip above water is your behaviour, what everyone sees—CEO Nisha, relentless, untouchable. But below the surface lies the bulk of the iceberg—patterns, beliefs, and conditioning that silently pull the strings. I'd heard this metaphor before, but in this workshop after my Hoffman Process experience, it landed differently, illuminated by a new light. Science backs this up: as children, we're wired for survival, utterly dependent on our parents for love, food, and safety. Unlike other animals that stand on their own within days or weeks, humans spend years in vulnerability. That dependency shapes us at deep levels.

Our early interactions with caregivers and our environment condition our actions. If a child learns that being tough or successful earns attention, they'll lean into that behaviour. Over time, those actions become automatic patterns—efficient shortcuts our brains use to navigate life. These patterns solidify into values, beliefs, and eventually the personality we present to the world. For me, it started young. As the firstborn after my parents lost a child, I was special, basking in my parents' love. But when my brother arrived, my mother's focus shifted to the new infant, and I turned to my dad. I craved his attention and molded myself to maintain it—becoming the tough, no-nonsense achiever, the winner. From a child's survival perspective, it made sense: If I'm the best, I'm loved. That became my identity, even when I no longer needed it.

The good news? This programming isn't permanent. Neuroplasticity—the brain's ability to rewire itself—means we can change these patterns. Like a sled carving a path down a snowy hill, our brains default to the familiar route because it's efficient. But with effort, we can forge a new path. It's tough at first, like trudging through fresh snow, but with practice, it becomes the new default. As with the Hoffman Process, this workshop also pointed to shadow work as the key—confronting those hidden drivers and redirecting their energy. That idea stuck with me: my patterns were energy, frozen in old shapes, but I could melt and reshape them.

Physiology and Emotions

Then they hit us with physiology and emotions, a concept grounded in science and experience. Your emotional state is tied directly to your body—change your physiology, and you change how you feel. Research in embodied cognition shows this: stand tall with your chest open, and confidence rises; slouch with shallow breaths, and you sink into gloom. I'd felt it in yoga—deep, slow breathing grounding me, shifting my energy from chaos to calm. The workshop framed it plainly: emotions are energy, and your body is the switch. Stand tall, breathe deep, and the fog lifts. Tense up, slump over, and you're trapped. It was logic I could grab—practical, not mystical—a tool to harness my energy in real time.

Filters and Triggers (Meta-Programs)

Filters and triggers came next, labeled as meta-programs from Neuro-Linguistic Programming (NLP), a psychological approach to communication and change. These are mental patterns that shape how we process the world. Some people focus on what's missing (scarcity mindset); others see what's present (abundance mindset). Examples include:

Towards/Away From: Are you motivated by chasing rewards or avoiding pain?

Internal/External Reference: Do you trust your own judgment or seek others' approval?

Global/Specific: Do you see the big picture or zoom in on details?

These filters set off triggers—experiences that spark an emotional reaction. For me, chaos or loss of control flipped a switch, sending my energy into overdrive. The workshop taught me to spot these patterns by asking: Why do I react this way? The answers weren't pretty—my tight wiring came from years of needing to prevail over uncertainty. Recognizing this was the first step to redirecting that energy, turning a reactive flare into a conscious choice.

Clare Graves' Levels of Consciousness

Then came Clare Graves' levels of consciousness, part of Spiral Dynamics, a model of human development. Graves, a psychologist in the 1950s, built his theory based on decades of observing how people adapt to complexity. Graves' core insight was that human consciousness evolves in response to changing life conditions, both individually and collectively. He saw individuals and societies moving through consciousness levels as they adapted to increasing complexity. Each level, signified by a colour, reflects a mindset and a way of being. For example, a person might shift from Orange (achievement-driven) to Green (community-focused) as their priorities change, just as societies evolve from Red (tribal warfare) to Blue (structured governance). He rejected rigid stages, proposing a spiral of development where each level includes and transcends the last. Later, Don Beck and

Christopher Cowan dubbed it Spiral Dynamics, but Graves' core insight remained.

Beige: Basic survival - Cave-dwellers scavenging to survive.

Purple: Tribal bonds, magical thinking - Tribes chanting around fires, bound by myth.

Red: Power, dominance - Warriors conquering; glory, their prize.

Blue: Order, tradition - Medieval societies with laws and gods.

Orange: Achievement, success(my old turf) - Industrialists and inventors, with wealth the goal.

Green: Community, equality(where I felt pulled) - Activists uniting for justice, hearts open.

Yellow: Integrative, systemic thinking - Thinkers linking systems, minds expansive.

Turquoise: Holistic, global awareness - Sages seeing earth as one, spirits whole.

Each level fits within its context—Blue's order tames Red's chaos, Orange's ingenuity lifts Blue's limits. Emotions mark the transitions: Red's anger tires into Blue's duty, Orange's pride empties into Green's care. Graves saw this as endless—new challenges spark new levels. Graves emphasized that individuals and societies can operate at different levels simultaneously, depending on context. For example, you might describe yourself as "straddling Orange and Green," which aligns with Graves' view that people can exhibit multiple levels or transition between them. This also applies to societies, where different groups or individuals may operate at different levels (e.g., a Blue-structured government coexisting with Orange-driven businesses). I was straddling orange and green during the workshop—restless with the grind of winning, craving deeper connection. This shift explained my itch, my energy seeking a new frequency beyond material success.

The Enneagram: A Mirror I Avoided

The Enneagram remained the workshop's heartbeat, but this wasn't the quick online quiz I'd aced before, spitting out "Type 8"—challenger, leader, maverick—based on my answers. This was a reflective process, splitting the nine personality types into triads (fear, anger, shame), centers (head, heart, gut), and styles (competency, outlook, intensity). We read descriptions, dug into ourselves, and chose our type and wings—no one handed us a label; we had to claim it.

I was dead-set on Type 8—anger-driven, gut-based, intense. But every step pointed to Type 2—heart-based, shame-fueled, nurturing. I hated it. The Helper description felt like a punch: giving, caring, connecting. I saw "servant," "weak," not the badass I'd built. I could be a 2w1 (idealistic) or 2w3 (ambitious), but I wanted the 8's power, not the 2's softness. The process was relentless, and my reflections screamed 2. I fought it—my heart still roared "challenger"—but the truth seeped through.

Here's the kicker: energy doesn't lie. A Type 2 falls into an 8's shadow when it denies itself. Reject the nurturer, and you get the controller—aggressive, disconnected. That was me, living in my shadow, suppressing my core. I was a 2w3—the 3's achiever energy had taken over, fueling "winner Nisha." The goal? Lean into my 2, balance the wings. I'd ditched my 1 wing (idealism) and buried my 2 (care), letting the 3 (success) run wild. It was an energy mismatch, and I felt it.

Shadow Integration: Digging Up the Roots

The shadow integration process was heavy. Shadow integration draws on the iceberg analogy and uses NLP tools to highlight and integrate our shadows. In Jungian psychology, shadows are the parts we repress—traits, emotions, desires we've deemed unacceptable, often from childhood. They don't vanish; they lurk, draining energy to stay hidden. Integration means dragging them into the light, owning them. As we sat with our eyes closed, tracing our shadows' roots, I saw little Nisha, craving my dad's approval, his empire towering over me. As I grew, I vowed to match him, building a wall of drive. No surprise there. But looking deeper, I saw empathy fade, walls thicken. Chasing that Type 8 shell, I'd traded connection for control. The softer me—giving, caring—was buried. The realization stung, but it was undeniable. The shell was cracking, and I felt it giving way to a greater power.

My core Type 2 had been in the shadow, a sacrifice to win my dad's love, to be the chosen one. It wasn't about titles or victories—it was a desperate grab for connection. Humans are wired for it, especially as kids. We're helpless for years, relying on our parents' gaze to survive. That need shapes us, crystallizes into patterns, becomes our iceberg's base. I'd molded myself for my dad, and that mold became me. But energy trapped in shadows doesn't rest—it festers. Facing it was the first step to freeing it.

Energy: The Hum Beneath It All

Day three zeroed in on energy, starting with Relationship Dynamics and masculine/feminine vibes. Relationship dynamics outlines six positions or stages relationships can cycle through—possibly echoing models like Susan Campbell's stages: romance, power struggle, stability, commitment, co-creation, and bliss. Stress in a relationship, the instructor said, comes from unmet needs, clashing energies, or lost polarity. The discussion shifted to Masculine and Feminine Energies, not about gender but universal forces we all carry. Masculine Energy is action, structure, logic—a driving force that pushes forward. Feminine Energy is flow, intuition, connection—a nurturing pull that holds space. The facilitator explained that attraction thrives on polarity: Masculine draws Feminine, and Feminine draws Masculine. When life, like my high-stakes business role, locked me into relentless Masculine drive, I lost my Feminine flow. Relationships frayed, my energy tipped out of balance. Seeing this as an energy imbalance, not a personal failing, flipped a switch. Masculine pushes—action, structure. Feminine pulls—flow, nurture. I'd been all push, no pull. This echoed therapist and Family Constellation founder, Bert Hellinger's perspective: feminine energy flows with intuitive connection, while masculine energy serves with purpose and direction.

To make this tangible, they split us into groups to demonstrate these energies. Men went up front, embodying the Masculine through breath and movement, while women sat to observe, perhaps to ground the Feminine in stillness. The exercise wasn't about steps or mechanics—it's something you have to feel to understand. The contrast was electric, the difference between Masculine and Feminine Energies so vivid and now easier to understand. Sitting there, still half-armored as a Type 8, I now recognized my Type 2's Feminine side—nurturing, soft. The exercise didn't change me; it brought into focus a truth I'd always known deep inside. I'd spent years rejecting Feminine Energy, equating its softness with weakness, its flow with loss of control. Yet, lately, I'd begun to let it in, unknowingly, through simple acts like preparing meals for my boys. Those moments—pouring care and nourishment into something as quiet as a shared meal—had cracked my rigidity, letting softness seep into my life. This wasn't about the act itself, but the energy behind it: giving, loving, creating space for connection. The retreat's exercise, with its vivid contrast of Masculine drive and Feminine flow, drove this home. It sealed a transformation already unfolding, showing me that nurturing isn't a surrender; it's a strength, a pulse of life I'd long pushed away but was now ready to claim.

The exercise revealed something that I now knew. I'd softened recently, cooking for my boys, embracing a slower rhythm, but this went deeper. Giving, I realized, isn't weakness; it's my strength. We ended with a meditation—eyes closed, breathing slowly—and a hum settled over me, soft and steady. It wasn't just sound; it was vibration, a pulse connecting us all.

The workshop's big revelation for me was this: everything is energy. I'd felt it before—chakra work in yoga, emotional releases in Hoffman—but my logical mind needed a framework. In yoga, prana is life-force, the energy flowing through us, shifted by breath and movement. Here, it clicked: emotions are energy, thoughts are energy, relationships are energy. When we block it—with tension, denial, control—it stagnates. When we release it—through awareness, breath, integration—it flows. That hum was my energy waking up, and I was tuning into a frequency I'd long ignored.

Reflections: Shedding What I'd Outgrown

Rabbi Abraham Twerski, a psychiatrist and Torah scholar, nailed it with, of all things, his lobster analogy. A lobster grows by shedding its shell when it gets too tight—a process sparked by discomfort. We're the same: challenges signal growth. That hit home. Books I'd skimmed—like Raja Yoga, where prana is defined as life's pulse, controlled through breath to shape reality—came back into focus. I'd dismissed Hinduism as rigid, but it's a method, not a rulebook. Shadow integration frames emotions as energy—release the energetic blocks to free yourself. Twerski's words tied it together: "The stimulus for the lobster to grow is that it feels uncomfortable." My Type 8 shell fit once, but I'd outgrown it. The business collapse, the void—they were my cue to shed what I'd outgrown. I'd tried to numb the discomfort with distraction and denial, but growth lives in the tension.

I'd never seen life as energy flowing before. I had the sense of zooming out, above the chaos of my life, and spotting the currents moving through it all—emotions, patterns, connections, all vibrating. Those three days didn't transform me into some enlightened sage—I'm still too unserious for that. I'd chased a dream, crashed when it fell apart. But all my learnings from the various workshops and my journey within had cracked my shell.

I paused and opened up to greater possibilities for expansion, not fully, but I was softer, shedding a tightness I hadn't yet been ready to recognize and embrace. The esoteric processes for looking within served as a map; my mind was the compass. Energy was calling, and I was finally listening.

SIGMUND FREUD'S ICEBERG MODEL

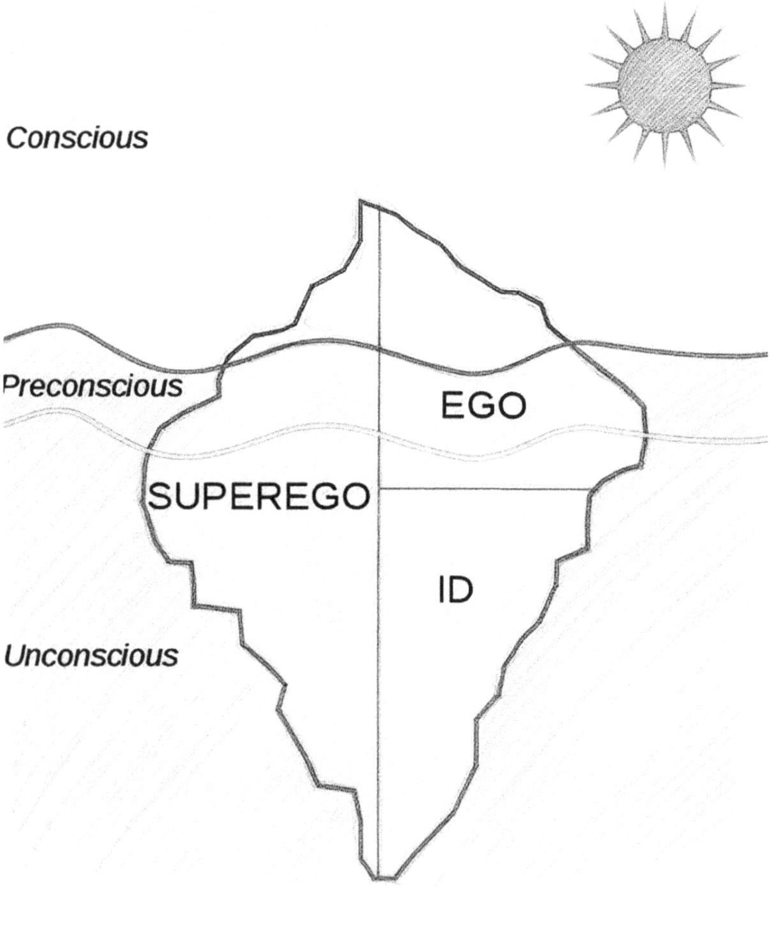

THE ENNEAGRAM

Take Action: Triad Spotlight

Your Enneagram type hides in your rhythms—shine a light on this. No checklists, just three lenses: emotion, center, style. What resonates most? Don't overthink it. Grab a pen and dive in.

Emotion Lens: Fear, Shame, Anger

Picture yourself at your lowest—cornered, exposed, raging. What's the gut-punch feeling you can't shake? Fear (dreading the unknown), shame (not enough), or anger (pushing back)? Describe the moment. Name the sensation.

Center Lens: Head, Heart, Gut

Recall the process of making a big decision. Where did it spark the greatest response? Head (logic), heart (connection), or gut (instinct)? Sketch the scene—what drove you forward? Circle the image that best illustrates your center.

Style Lens: Competency, Outlook, Intensity

When life hits hard, what's your response? Perfect it (competency), find the silver lining (outlook), or feel it all (intensity)? Remember a time when you were under pressure—how'd you roll? Describe your style.

Piece It Together

Got your trio? Fear + head + competency might be Type 5. Shame + heart + intensity could be Type 4. Check the appendix for type breakdowns. Pinpoint yours—does it fit?

One Last Look

Sit with it. What's the thread weaving through these reflections? Jot down one insight about yourself now.

No rush—this isn't a test. It's a mirror. See your reflection.

CHAPTER 5

EMOTIONS AS ENERGY – UNLOCKING THE PATH FORWARD

In Chapter 4, I introduced the idea that everything is energy—a realization that had dawned on me through years of yoga, meditation, and the subtle vibrations I'd felt in quiet moments, but which solidified during a transformative workshop. That shift reframed my world: a dynamic web of energies shapes our reality. Yet, even with this broader understanding, I found myself stuck. I'd traced my growth through Clare Graves' spiral dynamics, moving from Orange's ambition to Green's yearning for connection, and the Enneagram had unmasked me as a Type 2, not the Type 8 I'd thought I was. This awareness alone didn't propel me forward, however; I still needed to understand how to transform that restlessness into motion.

Then, by chance, I picked up a book left behind by a friend - "Power vs. Force" by David Hawkins, a renowned psychiatrist and researcher. Skeptical at first, I was drawn in by its clarity:

emotions aren't chaotic—they're energy in motion, each with a distinct frequency that governs our vitality and consciousness. This wasn't abstract philosophy; it was a practical bridge from feeling to action. Hawkins revealed that by engaging with emotions—especially the "higher" ones—we can tap into greater energy and unlock new paths. When I wove this into Graves' spiral and reflected on my own life, particularly during my experience with the Hoffman Process while grieving the passing of my son Arjun, the various approaches came together beautifully. This next chapter explores that nexus, using Hawkins' emotional scale, Graves' levels of consciousness, and the novel by Jean M. Auel, "The Clan of the Cave Bear," to elucidate how emotions and consciousness intertwine, culminating in my journey from grief to love and empathy.

Emotions as Energy: Hawkins' Revolutionary Framework

Chapter 4 established that energy is the foundation of existence—our bodies, thoughts, and surroundings all vibrate with it. Hawkins explores this further in his books, such as, "Power vs. Force" and "Letting Go," putting forth that emotions are a primary way this energy expresses itself. They're not mere reactions but forces with measurable frequencies that shape our physical health, mental clarity, and spiritual depth. He refers to them as "energy in motion"—a current that, when felt and released, lifts us, but when ignored or suppressed, drags us down.

The Map of Consciousness: A Detailed Emotional Spectrum

Hawkins' Map of Consciousness is his masterstroke—a numerical scale, from 1 to 1,000, that assigns values to emotions based on their energetic frequency. He developed it using kinesiology (explained later), but its power lies in its practicality. It's a method to decipher how emotions influence us from day to day. Let's explore each major emotional level in depth, with examples of how they play out in life:

Shame (20): The lowest rung—a crushing sense of worthlessness that saps every ounce of strength. It's the voice whispering that you're irredeemable, manifesting as social withdrawal or self-sabotage. Imagine someone who avoids eye contact, convinced they don't belong—shame drains their energy, leaving them weak and isolated.

Guilt (30): A step up but still heavy, laden with regret and self-blame. It's replaying a mistake—like snapping at a loved one—and feeling you can't undo it. Guilt traps people in cycles of "I should've done better," physically exhausting them with tension and sleepless nights.

Apathy (50): Numbness sets in here—a gray, listless detachment. It's the person who shrugs, "Nothing matters," staring blankly at a life they've checked out of. Apathy might look like someone slumped on a couch, unable to muster the will to move—energy is stagnant, hope a faint memory.

Grief (75): A deep, aching sadness, often tied to loss. It's the weight in your chest after a breakup or a death, a tender wound that casts a shadow over everything. Someone grieving might sit by a loved one's photo, tears welling up daily—it's natural, but lingering too long can become an isolating state of resisting change.

Fear (100): Restless and jittery, fear is the mind on high alert. It's worrying about a possible loss or imagining worst-case scenarios, heart racing at night. Fear narrows focus—think of someone pacing, unable to relax, their energy scattered by imagined threats.

Desire (125): A craving that pulls you forward but rarely fulfills. It's wanting a promotion, a new car, or approval, always chasing the next hit. Picture a shopaholic swiping their card yet again—desire drives action but leaves an empty buzz when the thrill fades.

Anger (150): Hot and sharp, anger lashes out or simmers within. It's yelling in traffic or resenting a perceived betrayal, fists clenched. Anger can spark change—like protesting against injustice—but unchecked, it burns out the person holding it, leaving exhaustion in its wake.

Pride (175): Ego's fragile crown, built on external props. It's boasting about a win or needing applause to feel good, only to crash when praise dries up. A proud person might strut after a promotion, but their energy teeters, as it is tied to others' opinions.

Courage (200): The turning point—a steady, quiet strength. It's saying "I'll try" despite doubts, like starting a new venture after failure. Someone courageous stands tall, not fearless but willing—energy shifts from draining to sustaining here.

Neutrality (250): A calm release of struggle, accepting life as it comes. It's shrugging off a setback. Lost a deal? Oh well, there is still a next time. Neutrality feels like taking a deep breath after a storm, invigorating energy flowing without resistance.

Willingness (310): An eager "yes" to life—openness to learn, connect, and grow. It's volunteering for a looming challenge or smiling at a stranger. Willingness radiates; think of a teacher staying late to help a student—the energy is active and generous.

Acceptance (350): At peace with reality, no railing against "what is." It's forgiving a flaw in yourself or others, like letting go of a grudge. Acceptance is a warm exhale—energy clarifies, decisions come easily.

Reason (400): Sharp, logical clarity—seeing cohesive patterns, solving puzzles. It's a scientist testing a hypothesis or a planner mapping a goal. Reason's energy is focused, potent, though it risks detachment without emotional warmth.

Love (500): A radiant, boundary-dissolving connection. It's hugging a child or helping a friend, no strings attached. Love feels expansive—energy soars, drawing others in with its attractive glow.

Joy (540): Light, bubbling gratitude for being alive. It's laughing at a sunrise or dancing for no reason. Joy lifts everything—energy sparkles, infectious to all who encounter it.

Peace (600): Inner stillness, characterized by a profound sense of unity with all of existence. It's meditating by a river, feeling part of the whole. Peace is quiet power—energy rests, yet resonates deeply.

Enlightenment (700-1000): Beyond most of us—a selfless, transcendent awareness. Think of a sage like the Dalai Lama, serene amid chaos. Energy here is limitless, one with the source.

Hawkins splits up the scale into "force" (below 200)—emotions like shame and fear that weaken us, rooted in survival—and "power" (200 and up)—emotions like courage and love that strengthen us, fostering growth. Our baseline emotion sets our energy level, attracting matching experiences: fear breeds tension, love draws harmony. Moving up requires feeling and releasing the lower states—grief can't be bypassed, only processed to reach acceptance.

How Hawkins Measured Emotional Range: Kinesiology Explained

How did Hawkins derive these numbers to create an emotional scale? Through kinesiology, a method based on applied kinesiology where muscle strength correlates with the body's response to various stimuli. Positive inputs—like truth or love—make muscles resist pressure; negative ones—like lies or fear—weaken them. Hawkins tested thousands of individuals, finding consistent patterns of response: "love" (at 500) always strengthened, "guilt" (at 30) always weakened. Science may scoff, but I felt its truth—anger left me shaky, love left me steady. The numbers are a guide; the real takeaway is that emotions are energy we can harness.

Letting Go: A Practice for Raising Energy

This was a great theory on emotions and their frequential levels. But, again, what to do with this information? In his book, "Letting Go," Hawkins offers a practical approach: emotions must be felt fully to be released. Suppression locks them in, sapping us; surrender frees them, lifting us. It's simple but can be subtle and nuanced—no need for theatrics to be effective. Here's the process he laid out:

Name It: Pinpoint the feeling of discomfort—anger, sadness—without shame.

Feel It: Let it sit in your body—tight chest, racing pulse—don't try to run from or suppress it.

Release It: Stop resisting; let it flow out like water through your fingers.

Shift Up: Watch higher emotions—calm, relief—rise naturally.

It might be a silent moment—breathing through a pang—or a written note letting guilt dissolve. I'd bottled emotions for years, thinking control was strength. Hawkins showed me it's the opposite: letting go is power, unblocking energy allows you to climb the emotional scale.

Consciousness Evolving: Clare Graves' Spiral Dynamics

We've explored Hawkins' map as a way to understand how emotions carry measurable energy frequencies that shape our state of being. But emotions don't just fluctuate within us — they also propel the evolution of our collective and individual consciousness. To see this, we can place Hawkins' scale alongside Clare Graves' Spiral Dynamics. Hawkins maps emotional energy; Clare Graves' spiral dynamics (Chapter 4) charts how consciousness expands with increasing emotional awareness.

Where Hawkins measures *vibration* — the energetic quality of our emotions — Graves maps *evolution* — the stages through which our awareness and values expand. When viewed together, these frameworks reveal that every emotional shift not only changes our inner state but also moves us through different worldviews. Emotion becomes the fuel that drives our climb up the spiral of consciousness.

Graves saw human development as a spiral of levels, each with distinct values and worldviews, a way of adapting to life's demands. Emotions fuel this climb—here's how these two systems align:

Beige (Survival): Pure instinct—eat, sleep, live. Emotions: shame (20), guilt (30), apathy (50). Energy is primal, barely above collapse, focused only on survival.

Purple (Tribal): Focus on group safety, safety through belonging and rituals. Emotions: fear (100), desire (125). Energy bonds the clan, still low and reactive.

Red (Power): Ego unleashed—dominate or be dominated. Emotions: anger (150), pride (175). Energy is raw, impulsive, explosive, driven by assertion.

Blue (Order): Rules, authority, and duty provide meaning and stability. Emotions: courage (200), Neutrality (250). Energy is controlled, rigid, enforcing structure and law.

Orange (Achievement): Rationality, competition, and innovation drive success. Emotions: pride (175), desire (125), willingness (310). Energy is ambitious, restless, striving—focused on results and progress.

Green (Community): Connection, empathy, equality, and shared values. Emotions: love (500), acceptance (350). Energy is warm, connective, humanistic, valuing relationships.

Yellow (Systems): Integrative, big-picture thinking, adaptability. Emotions: reason (400), neutrality (250). Energy is clear, versatile, able to hold paradox and complexity.

Turquoise (Holistic): Oneness with all, global consciousness, holistic unity. Emotions: peace (600), joy (540), enlightenment (700-1000). Energy is vast, serene, transcendent, non-dual awareness.

Emotions Driving the Spiral

Emotions aren't side effects; they're the sparks. Red's rage pushes for power, but its fallout births Blue's restraint. Orange's wins feel hollow, nudging Green's compassion. Hawkins quantifies it: below 200, we're stuck in survival (Beige to Blue); above, we connect and create (Green to Turquoise). My Orange-to-Green shift needed grief (75) to yield to love (500)—emotions were the ladder. My path, from Chapter 5, went from Orange's drive to Green's pull for connection. Hawkins clarified why: Orange's pride (175) powered my career but faltered under loss. Green's love (500) required clearing deeper emotions first. Emotions are the ladder to higher consciousness because they are also the ladder to intelligence itself. The more deeply we feel, the more widely we perceive—and in that expanded perception, both awareness and intelligence grow together. This truth isn't just philosophical; it's etched in our very evolution.

A Story in Stone: The Clan of the Cave Bear

I've always found that ideas come alive when we can feel them in tangible ways. Theories explain how consciousness evolves, but stories show us what that looks like in motion. One story that captures this perfectly is Jean Auel's The Clan of the Cave Bear which has stayed with me since my teens, not only for its vivid prehistoric world but for the question it awakened in me. The novel imagines a time when two human species—the Neanderthal and the Cro-Magnon—coexisted. When I first read it, that idea fascinated me because it went against what we were taught then: that one species disappeared before the other began. Only later would science confirm what Auel seemed to sense intuitively—that these two kinds of humans did, in fact, share space, even interbreed, and likely exchanged both tools and feelings.

In the story, Ayla, a young Cro-Magnon girl, is orphaned by an earthquake and found by a Neanderthal clan. She grows up among them, loved yet never fully accepted. The Clan lives by instinct and ritual. Their world is built on survival, tradition, and fear of the unknown. Ayla's world is different. She feels deeply—grief for her lost family, love for her adoptive mother, courage to defy their laws, curiosity that drives her to invent and heal. Her emotions disturb the Clan precisely because they cannot recognise them. When she weeps, they think she is ill; when she creates, they think she is dangerous.

As a teenager I saw this simply as a story about intelligence—Ayla as the more advanced, clever human who could innovate while the Clan could not. But reading it again years later through Hawkins' map of energy and Graves' spiral of consciousness, I realised that what truly differentiates them is not intellect alone—it is emotion. The Clan's narrow range of feeling keeps their awareness locked at the survival levels of fear and apathy—what

Hawkins places below 200. Ayla's emotional breadth—her grief, courage, and love—propels her upward through those frequencies into willingness, acceptance, and even love. Her emotions are not weaknesses to be controlled; they are engines of awareness that open her mind, ignite creativity, and expand consciousness itself. The Clan's limited emotions—fear and apathy—lock their consciousness in survival, their inability to express grief stifling imagination. Ayla's expressive range—grief through tears, courage, love—unlocks higher awareness, enabling innovation and connection the Clan cannot achieve. Her tears, a release of grief, allow her to climb the emotional ladder, from low to high vibrations, driving her evolution. This clarified for me: consciousness hinges on emotional expression, not just thought. The Clan stagnates, unable to express or move beyond limited emotions; Ayla evolves, her expressive breadth opening new possibilities. History mirrors this: from survival-driven early humans (Beige) to tribal traditions (Purple), rule-bound empires (Red/Blue), innovative modernity (Orange), and empathetic movements (Green)—each step fueled by expanding emotional expression.

Modern research supports what Auel's fiction intuited. Studies in evolutionary psychology show that emotional capacity evolved hand-in-hand with intelligence. As social groups grew more complex, humans who could recognise and respond to emotions—both their own and others'—had a greater chance of surviving and thriving. Emotional awareness became a selective advantage, enabling cooperation, empathy, and learning. In other words, our capacity to feel widely and deeply may have been the very catalyst for the evolution of our thinking.

Seen through this lens, The Clan of the Cave Bear is more than historical imagination—it is a mirror for human evolution. The Clan represents emotional repression and stagnation; Ayla embodies emotional expansion and growth. Her tears mark the moment consciousness begins to evolve beyond mere survival. Emotion, once dismissed as primitive, becomes the bridge to higher intelligence and deeper humanity.

We often imagine that life would be easier if we could simply think without feeling, that emotions get in the way of clarity. Yet Ayla's story shows the opposite: it is our emotional range—the willingness to feel grief, love, wonder—that fuels the very evolution of mind and spirit. Feeling is not the obstacle to our becoming; it is the path itself.

I share this because it made these ideas real, shifting my skepticism to curiosity as I saw Ayla's expressive emotions reflect my own search. The Clan and Ayla mirror our potential: by expressing our full emotional range, like Ayla's tears of grief, we climb the emotional ladder, expanding consciousness beyond survival to a higher state of being.

My Journey: Grieving Arjun, Finding Flow

How does this connect to my story? When Arjun died, I buried my grief, believing I could outrun it by diving into work and parenting my other sons. I thought I was strong, but Hawkins' scale revealed the cost: by not expressing my grief (75), I let it fester below 200, draining my energy. Plans stalled, joy faded—not from lack of will, but from the emotional gridlock of unexpressed grief, locking me from the flow Ayla found through her tears.

My experience with The Hoffman Process, during the week-long retreat described in Chapter 3, broke that dam. It wasn't one big release but a slow thaw, achieved through exercises designed to expose what I'd dodged. On day One, we visualized lost loved ones. I saw Arjun's bright eyes, his toddler grin. I spoke to him silently: I miss you. I'm sorry I couldn't save you. Tears came, soft but steady, and I let them. Another task had us write letters: one to Arjun, spilling my love and guilt; another to myself, forgiving my limits. Hawkins' process of letting go unfolded—I felt the grief's weight, its ache in my ribs, and released it, breath by breath.

At The Hoffman Process, each day peeled back another layer. Monday, guilt (30) for not being enough; Tuesday, anger (150) at the course of fate; Wednesday, fear (100) of more loss. We used tools—journaling, guided talks, even hitting pillows to move stuck energy—but for me, it was an internal practice. I'd sit by a window, naming the feeling, letting it pass. By Friday, love (500) crept in—not forced, but natural, like sun after rain. I felt it for Arjun, my boys, even myself. Empathy followed, softening my Type 2 walls.

The facilitators framed it simply: Feel it to free it. One exercise had us list what we carried—mine was "Arjun's death, my failure." We tore those papers, burned them in a fire pit, watching smoke rise. It wasn't magic, but it shifted me. I left lighter, energy unstuck, climbing from 75 to 500. Post-Hoffman, I kept at it.

Driving home, I'd hear a song Arjun loved and let the pang hit—no pushing it down. At night, I'd recall his laugh, feel the loss, and release it. Each moment freed energy, aligning with Hawkins: emotions in motion raise frequency. Graves' Green, representing connection and care, opened as I cleared the blockages. By allowing myself to remember our moments together—his smile, our shared joy—I faced the pain of grief, freeing the energy I'd suppressed to avoid it, honoring Arjun through love. I'd replayed holding him, helpless, blaming myself. Hoffman let me see: I'd done my best. Releasing that guilt wasn't a process of forgetting him—it was honoring him with love instead of pain.

Beyond Me: The Universal Thread

This isn't just my story—it's everyone's. Grief, loss, or stress touch us all—a parent gone, a job lost, a home uprooted. Hawkins' Scale of Consciousness maps our path: from shame (20) to courage (200) to peace (600). Graves' spiral frames this as growth itself—each emotional step lifts our vibration. Yet, under stress, we often fall into fight, flight, or freeze. The fight, flight, or freeze responses are primal survival mechanisms triggered by stress, each corresponding to distinct emotional states and energetic levels on David Hawkins' Scale of Consciousness. These responses, rooted in the autonomic nervous system, reflect how we cope with perceived threats, and their alignment with Hawkins' scale provides insight into their energetic impact on our lives. Fight, often associated with anger, resonates at a higher energetic level (around 150 on Hawkins' scale), where individuals confront challenges with assertive energy. Flight, tied to fear, vibrates slightly lower (around 100), reflecting avoidance driven by anxiety. Freeze, linked to shame, sits at a lower energetic frequency (around 20), characterized by paralysis and disconnection, as the individual withdraws inward, unable to act. These responses, while protective, can trap us in low-energy states, hindering our climb to higher consciousness and our evolution.

Dr. Gabor Maté, a physician and trauma expert known for his work on how early experiences shape lifelong behaviors, offers insight here. In books like The Myth of Normal, Maté argues that childhood environments where emotional needs are unmet—through neglect, rejection, or loss—condition us to adopt survival responses like fight, flight, or freeze. For instance, when a child's healthy anger is punished or their fear ignored, they may internalize coping mechanisms that limit their emotional range under stress. He writes, "The personality we develop is not a reflection of our true selves, rather a defense against the loss of love". This conditioning can lock individuals into repetitive patterns, where stress triggers one of these three responses rather than a broader spectrum of emotional possibilities. Over time, these patterns become rigid, reinforcing a cycle where the body and mind default to fight, flight, or freeze, even when the situation calls for a more nuanced response.

Each of us tends to gravitate toward a primary response shaped by both conditioning and personality. In the framework of the Enneagram, these tendencies align with core emotional drivers. As an Enneagram Type 2, a "Heart Triad" type driven by feelings, my default response under stress is often to freeze. This manifests as a momentary paralysis, where I withdraw to avoid rejection or to manage feelings of unworthiness, a hallmark of Type 2's struggle with self-worth. However, past conditioning or situational triggers can sometimes push me toward flight (avoiding conflict to preserve relationships) or fight (asserting myself to prove my value). This variability underscores Maté's point that our responses are not fixed but are heavily influenced by learned patterns from our past.

Maté's work shows how such conditioning can limit our emotional range, keeping us cycling through low-energy responses. The Hoffman Process, described earlier, helped me break this cycle by feeling and releasing shame, guilt, and fear, climbing toward love (500). This pattern echoes universally: a nation post-war, shifting from fight (anger, 150) to acceptance (350), rebuilding with hope. Emotions, when felt and released, become our alchemy, transforming pain into higher consciousness.

Summarizing the Path of Emotional Development

Chapter 4 established that everything is energy; this chapter shows emotions as our tool to wield it. Hawkins' scale reveals each feeling's vibration—low ones like shame (20) or fear (100) drag us down, high ones like love (500) or joy (540) uplift. Graves' spiral maps our climb, each level an emotional milestone. The Clan of the Cave Bear illustrates this through Ayla, whose love transcends the Clan's fear. My grief for Arjun taught me that releasing pain didn't erase him—it freed me to honor him with love, not burden.

Hawkins' premise is clear: higher emotions unlock higher energy, but we must feel authentically, not force it. Stress often locks us in fight (anger, 150), flight (fear, 100), or freeze (shame,

20), shaped by conditioning that Maté urges us to question: "Why am I reacting this way? Do I need to?". As a Type 2, I'm learning to notice my freeze response, feel the shame beneath, and let it pass, opening to courage (200) or love (500). We clear lower emotions—grief, guilt, fear—by feeling them fully, as I did in The Hoffman Process, not by fighting or fleeing. Graves adds: this is humanity's arc, from survival to unity. Explore Power vs. Force or Graves' spiral for deeper insight, but start simply: name your response—fight, flight, or freeze—feel its root, and release it. That's the path forward and upward—flow, not force.

Take Action: Feel, Map, and Move Forward

This exercise helps you apply the chapter's insights to your own life by connecting your emotional state to your level of consciousness and taking a small step toward growth. It's simple, reflective, and designed for gradual progress—no pressure, just awareness and action.

1. Name Your Current Emotion

What to Do: Think of a recent moment that stirred a strong feeling—maybe frustration, joy, or sadness. Choose one word that sums up your dominant emotion as you consider that moment (e.g., anger, peace, shame).

Why: Emotions are energy in motion, and naming them helps you see where you're starting on the emotional scale.

2. Place It on Hawkins' Scale

What to Do: Refer to Hawkins' Map of Consciousness from the above chapter. Where does your emotion fall? Below 200 (e.g., fear at 100, guilt at 30) or above (e.g., courage at 200, joy at 540)? If unsure, consider: Does this emotion feel heavy or light?

Why: Pinpointing your emotional energy level reveals how it's influencing your perspective.

3. Map Your Consciousness Level

What to Do: Reflect on your current mindset and priorities. Which Graves' spiral level fits you today?

Beige: Survival, basic needs.
Purple: Tradition, family, or group loyalty.
Red: Power, independence, or impulse.
Blue: Order, rules, or purpose.
Orange: Success, achievement, or reason.
Green: Community, empathy, or equality.
Yellow: Systems, flexibility, or big-picture thinking.
Turquoise: Unity, peace, or holistic awareness.
Why: Your consciousness level shapes how you experience and express emotions.

4. Identify the Itch or Pull

What to Do: Ask yourself: Am I restless or stuck? Do I sense a quiet nudge toward something more,like freedom, connection, or peace?
Example: In Blue (order), you might feel drawn to Orange (success). In Green (community), you might crave Yellow (systems).
Why: This restlessness often signals readiness to evolve.

5. Peek at the Next Level

What to Do: Look at the next Graves' level up. What emotions might come with it?
Red to Blue: From anger (150) to courage (200).
Orange to Green: From pride (175) to love (500).
Green to Yellow: From acceptance (350) to reason (400).

Why: Seeing the emotional shift can effectively guide your growth.

6. Feel the Pull

What to Do: Tune in. Do the emotions of the next level call to you, even faintly? Imagine what it would feel like to embody them.
Example: If in Red, does Blue's sense of purpose stir something in you?
Why: This pull is your inner guidance calling you toward a higher state.

7. Take One Small Step

What to Do: Pick a tiny action that matches the higher emotion and consciousness level you're drawn toward.
Toward Blue (courage): Speak up about something small.
Toward Green (love): Send a kind message to someone.
Toward Yellow (reason): Explore a new idea or question.
Why: Small steps build momentum and align your energy with growth.

8. Reflect

What to Do: After you take action, check in with yourself. How do I feel now? Did my energy shift? Revisit this process whenever you need clarity or a boost.
Why: Growth is a spiral, and each step counts.

CHAPTER 6

HEALING THE FORM – RELEASING THE ENERGY

The Enneagram workshop described in Chapter 4 cracked my shell open. I'd lived as a Type 8—bold, unyielding, the rock everyone leaned on, only to find that I was a Type 2 underneath, a giver who'd hidden her own needs within a fortress of strength. It was disorienting, like waking up in someone else's life. The years had already battered me: the family business collapsing, the unbearable void left by my son Arjun's death, my husband's betrayal slamming the door on any trust I had left. These weren't just wounds I held in my mind—they'd etched themselves into my body. My shoulders slumped under an invisible load, my chest tightened with a dull ache, and a discordant hum vibrated in my bones. My experience as described in Chapter 3 had sparked something—chakra meditations stirring energy, breathwork quieting my chaos, the Hoffman Process unleashing a torrent of tears—but those were fleeting glimpses, not the deep shift I craved. I needed more than temporary relief. I needed to unravel this tangle of pain and energy, to satisfy the part of me that demands evidence, not just a belief.

That's when David Hawkins' "Power vs. Force" had found me. His mapping of emotions as energy frequencies—shame dragging at 20, grief weighing in at 75, lifting to love at 500 wasn't abstract; it was a framework I could test out, a guide to where I was stuck and how I could rise. This wasn't some ethereal notion, energy isn't a ghost floating above us; it lives in the body. Emotions don't just swirl in our heads, they sink into our muscles, our nerves, our cells. After Arjun's death, I didn't break down or scream—I armoured up, buried the grief in my work, and let a heavy silence swallow the rest. The Hoffman Process had pried open my armour, letting love peek through, but a stubborn block remained, a physical weight I couldn't shake. Then I stumbled across Donny Epstein, a chiropractor who saw the body as a vault of trapped emotions, and it all clicked: healing isn't just a mental game—it's physical, rooted in the energy we carry.

The Mind-Body Connection: Emotion as Physical Force

We've all heard the dismissive phrase: "It's all in your head." That's a half-truth at best. Emotions don't stay confined to the mind—they move through the body with visceral power. Anxiety clamps your chest, races your heart, grinds your teeth. Anger ignites your stomach and flushes your face. Grief settles into your shoulders like lead. These aren't metaphors—they're realities you can feel. Science has caught up to what healers have known all along: emotions are biological events. In the 1990s, neuroscientist Candace Pert discovered that emotions show up as peptides—chemical messengers that course through the body, binding to receptors and altering how our systems function. For instance, fear triggers a surge of adrenaline, preparing us to react, while joy releases endorphins, easing us into calm. Pert's key insight was that these peptides don't just pass through; they can become embedded in our cells, archiving unprocessed emotions as physical traces that linger and influence our physiology long after the initial experience.

Try it yourself. Think of a time when you were furious—your fists ball up, your jaw tightens, heat surges in your chest. Now recall a moment of pure love—your shoulders relax, your breath deepens, warmth spreads. These responses aren't quirks; they're universal. The body doesn't whisper—it speaks, loudly and clearly, if we'd only listen.

For years, I had ignored that voice. After Arjun died, I didn't let myself fall apart. No tears, no outbursts—I squared my shoulders, drowned the pain in endless tasks, keeping the threat of flooding emotions at bay. But my body didn't forget. My back became rounded, my chest pulsed with a quiet, persistent ache—a testament to the sorrow I'd refused to face. I thought I'd outrun it, but I'd only buried it deeper. We dismiss these signals until they roar—migraines that mock rest, exhaustion that defies sleep. The body responds quickly, but we're often too distracted or too stubborn to understand the body's connection to buried emotions.

Masaru Emoto's water experiments offer a provocative angle. He claimed that emotions could imprint on water. Words like "love" or "peace" formed elegant, symmetrical crystals when frozen, while "hate" or "fear" twisted them into chaotic shards. Skeptics scoff, calling it pseudoscience, but the concept lingers: if emotions can leave a mark on water, and we're 70% water, what might decades of suppressed grief or rage do to our own structure? It's not definitive proof, but it's cause to wonder. Could unvoiced emotions distort our cells, our energy, our very essence?

Rigorous scientific research offers firmer ground. In the 2000s, biologist Bruce Lipton explored epigenetics, demonstrating that chronic stress from emotions like anger, fear, or shame can alter gene expression. In simple terms, epigenetics refers to how your behaviors and environment can cause changes that affect the way your genes work. Unlike genetic changes (mutations), epigenetic changes are reversible and do not change the sequence of DNA bases, but they can change how your body reads a DNA sequence. This process involves flipping genetic switches that dictate how our genes function, potentially affecting our health over time. Lipton's work suggests that these persistent negative emotions don't simply fade—they reshape our biology by modifying how our genetic code is expressed. The HeartMath Institute, since the '90s, has demonstrated that emotions influence heart rhythms. Calm states create smooth, coherent patterns, while frustration or anxiety generate chaotic beats. Emotions aren't fleeting thoughts—they're forces, molding us from the inside out.

Emotions as Energy: A Framework I Could Grasp

Chapter 5 set the stage: emotions are energy we can feel, a bridge to the invisible. This hooked me because I'm not one for blind faith—I echo the call Swami Vivekananda, to test every philosophy or belief against experience. I need to examine it, feel it, and then share it to own it. Emotions gave me an entry point—something tangible to understand the unseen.

When I'm angry, I can feel blood pulsing through my temples; when I feel love, I can feel my chest expanding. You might sense it elsewhere—your gut, your throat—but we all know emotions land in the body. The more I pay attention, the sharper the experience becomes. It's not just in the present moment, either; it is also true for our memories. Think back to a time when you were enraged—your muscles tense again, don't they? Recall love, and that glow creeps back. This isn't woo-woo; it's palpable, a mind-body connection we can touch. For me, it's the first step to getting a handle on energy.

If emotions are energy, and energy needs to move, what happens when it doesn't? Like water in a pipe—block it, and the pressure builds until it bursts. Unexpressed or unprocessed emotions work the same way. They don't dissipate; they accumulate, embedding in the body—along the spine, in the muscles, in the breath. This is where pioneers like Donny Epstein, a chiropractor who developed Network Spinal Analysis, as well as Reiki practitioners, and yoga teachers step in. They see the body as a map of these blockages, offering tools to free the flow.

The Science of Storage: How Emotions Take Root

To grasp how emotions get trapped, look at the nervous system. The spine, a conduit of nerves, is the body's communication hub. When we suppress emotions, we don't just bottle feelings—we create tension patterns that warp this pathway over time, like a river etching a gorge. The body adjusts, but it pays a price: energy that should flow freely gets locked, leading to misalignment, discomfort, or emotional deadness.

If emotions are held down—they stack up, lodging in the body like clutter in a storeroom. Healers have long acknowledged it: unprocessed emotions knot the shoulders, stiffen the spine, shallow the breath. For years, I carried this record in my back. It was a physical vestige of the grief and anger I'd brushed aside. I didn't connect the dots until I dug into this: these weren't random pains; they were emotional blockages. Left unchecked, this buildup can spiral—chronic pain, illness, breakdowns that finally force us to face what's buried. Psychosomatic research backs this up. A study in the Journal of Psychosomatic Research found that unresolved trauma often correlates with chronic conditions like fibromyalgia or migraines. The body becomes a living ledger of our emotional past, storing what we won't release.

Lower-Frequency Emotions: The Weight We Carry

Emotions vibrating at lower frequencies—shame, guilt, fear, grief—don't just pass through; they settle in, layering like silt in a stream. Hawkins' scale puts numbers to it: shame at 20 collapses you, guilt at 30 chains you, apathy at 50 numbs you, grief at 75 drags you down, fear at 100 tightens its grip, anger at 150 smolders. Below 200, these emotions drain your energy, locking you in survival mode. Above 200—courage, love, peace—they fuel you, opening the door to growth. But the lower states, if repressed or expressed wrongly, clog the system, choking off access to the higher ones.

Looking back, I realize I wasn't always stuck in those lower states. I'd laugh with my sons, savor a hard-won deal, but the good feelings never lasted. Joy faded, and that chest tightness stayed. My husband's betrayal was devastating. I didn't collapse—no tantrums, no tears. I held steady, kept control. But inside, anger simmered, unvoiced. I didn't let it out; it wasn't my way. Yet suppressing it built a wall—my energy dulled, my focus blurred. It was as if I was trapped in a cycle of low-frequency emotions, unable to access the higher states of joy and peace. I realized I had been hoarding emotions like anger and grief, which, according to Hawkins' scale, vibrate at lower frequencies. These emotions drained my energy, keeping me in survival mode, far from the higher frequencies of love (500) or peace (540).

Science supports this mind-body connection. Candace Pert's research shows that emotions like anger trigger the release of cortisol, a stress hormone that can linger in the body if not properly released. Bruce Lipton's work on epigenetics suggests that prolonged exposure to low-frequency emotions can even alter gene expression, anchoring us in those states. For me, suppressing anger didn't just affect my mood; it impacted my entire being, creating a silent barrier to joy and growth. It was a powerful lesson in how our emotions, when not fully felt and released, can weigh us down, preventing us from rising to higher levels of consciousness and well-being.

But here's the good news: if emotions can get stuck, they can also move. This isn't a modern revelation—ancient wisdom and new methods align on this. Network Spinal Analysis, Reiki, yoga—all target trapped energy, each with its own approach.

They don't create healing; they release trapped emotions from the body.

Donny Epstein's Breakthrough: NetworkSpinal and the Network Spinal Wave

Donny Epstein, brought a revolutionary perspective to chiropractic care. He views the body as a repository of emotional history, etched into the spine and nervous system. In his book "The 12 Stages of Healing", he maps a journey from entrapment to freedom—not by masking pain, but by restoring flow. In Stage 1, Suffering, we are consumed by pain, and our energy is stuck in the body, unable to flow freely. Stage 2, Polarities, involves recognizing the internal conflict—blaming oneself or others, which further divides our energy. By Stage 3, Stuck in Illusion, we feel like victims, powerless to change, and our energy remains frozen. The early stages—Suffering, Polarities—reflect a reality where pain dominates and energy stalls. Higher stages—Freedom, Resolution—promise release and awareness.

Epstein developed Network Spinal Analysis (NSA), a chiropractic technique that uses precise, gentle touches to specific points on the spine to trigger the body's natural release of tension. Unlike traditional chiropractic, which often involves manual adjustments to correct spinal misalignments, NSA focuses on stimulating the body's innate ability to heal itself. Practitioners observe subtle cues in posture, muscle tension, and breathing to identify areas of stored tension or disrupted energy flow—often linked to emotional or physical stress. These areas, or blockages, are then gently touched to encourage the body to release the tension, rather than forcing a correction.

What makes Epstein's work unique is the Network Spinal Wave, a visible, wave-like ripple along the spine that emerges during NSA sessions. Epstein was the first to observe and document this phenomenon in chiropractic care, identifying it as a unique oscillation that reorganizes the nervous system through both electromagnetic and mechanical means. This wave is classified as a Central Pattern Generator (CPG)—a neural circuit that produces rhythmic patterns without ongoing external input, like those that drive walking or breathing. While CPGs are a recognized phenomenon in neuroscience, Epstein's discovery is groundbreaking: the Network Spinal Wave is the first CPG identified in the spine that doesn't rely on locomotion. Instead, it arises from gentle spinal stimulation, revealing the spine's innate ability to self-organize and release stored tension in a way previously unseen.

Epstein applied this discovery to NSA by using the wave to unlock energy trapped by emotional stress in the spine. Lower emotions, like fear or guilt, pile up in our body—especially along the spine—like silt clogging a pipe. This buildup blocks higher emotions, like joy or love, from flowing through us. Systems like NSA or Reiki give us outside help to clear these clogs. In NSA, a chiropractor uses a light touch at the right spot to start the spinal wave, a natural movement the body creates on its own. This wave acts like water flushing out a blockage, washing away the stuck emotions. The body "self-corrects" here, meaning it uses its own spinal wave to heal itself once the touch gives it a nudge. Why is this important? Without the clog, emotions would flow smoothly, but when they're stuck, we stay trapped in the lower feelings causing the blockage. Flushing the system lets the body open up to higher emotions and move to the next level. If we don't clear these emotional blockages, we're stuck in survival mode, feeling only the lower emotions that weigh us down. By using NSA to flush them out, we give our body a chance to heal and let higher emotions—like peace or happiness—flow through, lifting us up.

A 2016 study in the Journal of Alternative and Complementary Medicine (Volume 22, Number 7, pp. 544–556), co-authored by Epstein, used surface electromyography (sEMG) to measure electrical activity during NSA sessions. The findings showed that the Network Spinal Wave enhances coherence between the sacrum and cervical spine, a marker of nervous system integration. This coherence reduces tension and boosts well-being, effectively "tuning" the body's natural rhythm—like clearing blocks from an instrument to restore its harmony.

The practical impact is substantial. A University of California, Irvine study of over 2,800 participants found that NSA, guided by Epstein's wave-based approach, reduced pain and stress while improving quality of life. Participants reported less pain, better sleep, and greater resilience—outcomes tied directly to the wave's effects in clinical settings.

Epstein's work bridges chiropractic and energy healing, blending scientific rigor with profound results. His discovery of the Network Spinal Wave and its application in NSA offers a new lens on how the spine can heal itself, setting the stage for transformative experiences—like the one I'll share next.

My Experience with Network Spinal: A Welcome Release

I wasn't sold on the idea of chiropractic, not at first. Energy pathways, spinal "entrainments"—it all sounded like New Age nonsense, the kind I'd normally roll my eyes at and dissect with logic later. But there I was, in a group session with one of Donny Epstein's practitioners, a trained chiropractor who'd studied under him. By this time, I'd hit a wall—years of grief, anger, and tension stacked up inside me like bricks, and nothing else had pried them loose. Out of curiosity, I'd watched videos of Epstein's work before showing up: people twisting, crying out, their bodies moving in ways that looked unhinged, almost theatrical. *Is this a cult? Am I about to embarrass myself?* - I wondered, my inner skeptic injecting itself into my thoughts. Still, the part of me that had survived loss—Arjun's death, a fractured marriage—prevailed.

The room had several padded tables lined up, soft light filtering through a window, a faint hum of anticipation from the handful of us there. It didn't feel like a yoga studio or a therapy session; it was its own strange thing. I watched carefully as the first attendee climbed on to the table,the practitioner moved with quiet confidence, explaining that Network Spinal wasn't about force. No loud cracks or deep-tissue prodding. Instead,these were light, precise touches along the spine, just enough to cue the body to release what it was holding. "Your nervous system knows what to do," she said, her voice calm but firm. "We're just waking it up."

A few minutes later, it was my turn. I was now lying face down, my breath tight in my chest. My mind was already arguing: *This is too gentle to have a meaningful effect. I need something* stronger to break through years of pain. The session started with her hovering hands just above my spine— a presence I could somehow feel, like a warm breeze brushing my skin. Then came the first touch, feather-light, on a spot near my lower back. "Anger and pain are here," she said, definitively, like she was reading from my bones. "A lot's stacked up."

Before I could process her words, my body responded. Another gentle press, and my spine arched upward, lifting me off the table in a sharp, involuntary curve. A sound ripped out of me—a raw, jagged cry I didn't plan or recognize. It wasn't just a sob; it was a wail, primal and unfiltered, like something caged deep inside had finally been released. Grief for Arjun flooded out—his absence, the hole it left. Anger followed, hot and sharp, at my ex-husband, at myself, at the world. My body twisted into a shape that felt like a warped yoga pose, hips tilting, shoulders rolling, guided not by me but by whatever this energy was.

I didn't stop to think. I couldn't. The practitioner remained steady, her hands occasionally brushing another point on my spine, each touch sparking a new wave. "Let it move," she said softly. "Your body's letting go." And it did. For minutes—maybe five, maybe ten, I lost track—my voice filled the room, tears streaked down my face onto the table, and my muscles stretched and shook. It was messy, loud, unglamorous. The pain I'd carried for years, layered along my spine like sediment, spilled out.

When it finally ebbed, I collapsed back onto the table, breathless and damp with sweat and tears. The room felt still, almost shockingly quiet after the storm I'd unleashed. I sat up slowly, my chest lighter, like someone had lifted a stone I'd been hauling around for years. My analytical side kicked in fast—Was that real? Did I just exaggerate it in my head?—but the evidence was there: my breath flowed more easily, my shoulders loosened. It wasn't a full unraveling of everything I had been carrying, but it was a start, a tangible shift I couldn't deny.

Looking back, I still don't fully get it. Part of me wants to chalk it up to placebo or emotional exhaustion. But the seeker in me—the one who's investigated healing through meditation, therapy, and every other promising tool I could find—knows it was more. That light touch along my spine unlocked something my body had been screaming to release.

Reiki also takes a softer tack, aiming for the same release. Reiki practitioners channel energy through their hands—sometimes touching, sometimes hovering—to dissolve blocks. This process uses no force; it invites energy to shift and flow. It's even subtler than Network Spinal, but it taps the same truth: stuck emotions stack up, and the body can let them go to significant beneficial effect.

Yoga's been a thread since Chapter 3's focus on breathwork. Asanas or poses involve twists and bends that stretch the body and also stimulate the release of blockages. In one class, a hip opener triggered tears—grief tucked in my joints, freed by the stretch. Yoga isn't just exercise; it opens channels, letting energy flow where it's been dammed. Less direct than Network Spinal, less gentle than Reiki, it still demonstrates that the body holds emotions and movement can release them.

Historical Roots: A Universal Insight

The link between emotions and how they are held by the body isn't a new idea. Ancient Chinese medicine correlates emotions to specific organs—anger with the liver, grief with the lungs—releasing the suppressed emotions through acupuncture or qigong. Yoga tied emotions to chakras, using breath and poses to balance them. Hippocrates, centuries back, saw emotions shaping health, urging the practice of engaging with harmony to allow healing. Even Egypt's healers used touch and vibrations (sound) to shift energy. These traditions don't contradict modern methods—they complement them, affirming that energy gets trapped and the body can free them.

The Shared Principle

What ties these approaches together? They all view the body as a vessel and hold that unprocessed emotions don't fade over time; they linger until addressed. Pert's peptides shows that emotions become embedded in cells as chemical messengers, lingering and influencing our physiology even after the feeling subsides; Lipton's epigenetics reveals that chronic negative emotions persist by altering gene expression, reshaping our biology with lasting effects. Epstein's touches, Reiki's energy, yoga's poses—all unstack and release that burden. These practices don't heal us—they let our bodies heal ourselves.

Releasing Without Help: The Power Within

The exciting revelation? We don't always need a guide to heal. The body and mind know what's stuck and how to release it—we just need to listen and act. David Hawkins' Letting Go and Donny Epstein's Network Spinal Analysis (NSA) approach the same goal—freeing trapped emotions—but in distinct ways. Hawkins teaches us to mentally surrender to emotions, feeling them fully to let them dissolve. Epstein uses gentle spinal touches to spark the Network Spinal Wave, flushing out emotional blockages physically. Both show that healing starts within. While practitioners like those trained in NSA or programs like the Hoffman Process can offer a powerful boost, especially when we're stuck, we can't outsource the process. The real work—acknowledging and releasing emotions—belongs to us.

For me, facing Arjun's loss wasn't dramatic. After years of locking my emotions away, the Hoffman Process uncovered and released deep emotional patterns, breaking the dam, letting my grief flow. Afterward, I simply let memories of Arjun surface, feeling the ache in my chest without pushing it away. No theatrics—just presence. By identifying the grief in my body and allowing it to move through me, the weight lifted. Love crept back—hugs with my sons grew warmer, conversations deepened. It wasn't a revelation, just a quiet shift. Acknowledging the grief unstuck it, letting energy flow freely, and joy found room.

This process isn't about outsourcing healing—it's about owning it. External tools and guides are invaluable when we're lost, but the power is ours when we take the first step. Hawkins' scale tracks the climb: from grief (75) to acceptance (350) to love (500). The body shifts as the mind does—neuroplasticity rewires us with each release. Even Emoto's water experiments echo this: change the emotion, change the form.

Building a Practice: A Daily Reset

The facilitator at the Enneagram workshop had said that we live in a world with nearly 4,000 words for emotions in the English language, yet most of us can barely name a handful—happy, sad, angry, scared. This gap keeps us stuck, unable to navigate the energy that shapes our lives. To bridge it, I developed a simple daily practice to recognize emotions by identifying, naming, and locating them in the body. This isn't about fixing or releasing emotions yet—it's about seeing them clearly, building the awareness that makes transformation possible. So mornings, I sit, eyes closed, scanning myself. Where's the tension?— Neck from a spat, stomach from a deadline? I name it—irritation, stress—breathe into it, let it ease. Some days, it's fast; on others, I linger, stretching or shaking it the feeling loose. It's not mystical or ethereal—it's deliberate and effective, rooting energy work in a daily habit.

For someone like me, who craves a rational approach, this model clicks. Energy isn't vague or nebulous—it's vibratory and frequential. Emotions we feel are stored in the body and freed with intent. No mystery; just a series of predictable steps, a practical method accessible to everyone. It's straightforward, not flashy or complex. No expertise required—just you and your body, aligned. This practice isn't just about relief—it's about what emerges and the heightened potential for joy. With grief lighter, I felt love again—the frost around my heart was now gone. With anger dispersed, I forgave—not my ex-husband, but myself for any perceived wrongdoing in the past. Energy released isn't just freedom; it's potential.

Why It Matters: Creating Space

But why clear these emotions? Epstein's answer is clear: to move up the emotional ladder. By releasing unexpressed emotions, individuals can shift from lower states like fear or anger to higher states like love or peace. This shift is not merely about feeling better; it's about accessing higher energy states that align with higher versions of one's purpose. Unexpressed emotions clog us, blocking energy of higher states of experience. We might taste joy or love, but not enough to soar. Hawkins' courage (200) or Epstein's Freedom Stage need fuel—more than fear or grief can provide. Naming what's stuck starts the melt; letting it go keeps it flowing. After Arjun's passing, I was tethered to my grief, gripped by fear. Letting the emotions rise allowed my creativity to flow and sparked new and innovative ideas, a new and lighter way of being in the world. But releasing the stuck emotions didn't just end with me, there was a ripple effect, beyond me. My sons felt it—our talks flowed more freely, less strained. A friend remarked that I seemed "less burdened." The effects are not just confined to my personal experience; it radiates outward and affects those around me. Energy freed in one individual has pervasive effects.

Energetic States, Emotions, and the Path to Higher Purpose

Donny Epstein's work was not just limited to NSA and clearing energy blockages through his chiropractic. In his book, The Seeker's Code, Donny Epstein introduces the concept of energetic states, which are levels of energy that influence our ability to achieve our highest potential and truest purpose. Epstein argues that to reach the ultimate expression of energy—or to fulfill our deepest purpose—we must access the highest energy states. He emphasizes that lower energy states limit our capacity to achieve higher goals; thus, our energy state must match the purpose we seek to fulfill. This idea resonates with the works of David Hawkins and Clare Graves, who both explored how emotions and energy levels shape human development and consciousness. By integrating Epstein's insights with Hawkins' emotional energy scale and Graves' evolutionary model, we can better understand how clearing unexpressed emotions through techniques like Network Spinal Analysis (NSA) allows us to ascend the emotional ladder, access higher energy states, and align with higher versions of our purpose.

Epstein's Energetic States and the Quest for Purpose

Epstein's framework in The Seeker's Code revolves around the idea that energy is the foundation of life, influencing everything from physical health to spiritual awareness. He describes various energetic states—ranging from basic survival energy to transcendent spiritual energy—and posits that our ability to achieve our truest purpose is directly tied to the energy state we inhabit. Lower energy states, such as those associated with fear or survival, limit our potential, while higher states, like love or unity, expand our capacity for growth and fulfillment. Epstein asserts that you cannot achieve higher goals from a lower energy state; instead, your energy state must align with the purpose you seek. This alignment is crucial for unlocking what he calls the "ultimate expression of energy," where individuals can live in harmony with their deepest calling.

By weaving together Epstein's energetic states, Hawkins' emotional energy levels, and Graves' evolutionary spiral, we arrive at a holistic understanding of personal development. Epstein's work emphasizes that our energy state must match our purpose; we cannot achieve higher goals from lower states. Hawkins provides a map, showing that higher emotional states like love or peace are essential for growth. Graves adds that emotional evolution drives us toward more complex, inclusive ways of being. Together, these frameworks suggest that clearing unexpressed emotions—through practices like NSA—allows us to ascend the emotional ladder, access higher energy states, and align with higher versions of our purpose. This synthesis offers a practical yet profound path: by attending to the body's stored emotions, we can free ourselves from lower energy states, embrace higher emotions, and step into the fullest expression of who we are meant to be. As Epstein might say, it's not just about healing—it's about awakening to the extraordinary.

The Experience: A Threshold Crossed

The Network Spinal Analysis (NSA) session lingers in my memory—not for its drama, but for its quiet power. A gentle touch sparked a wave, a ripple that flushed out emotional silt, clearing a path for energy to flow. But this was only a spark. The real transformation unfolded through internal work, guided by David Hawkins' Letting Go. NSA and Hawkins' approach tackle the same challenge—releasing trapped emotions—but in different ways: NSA clears physical blockages with a spinal wave, while Letting Go asks us to name, feel, and release emotions from within. Both taught me that healing is our own.

Emotions, especially the heavy ones, layer like sediment in the body, clogging our spine and spirit. Shame, fear, grief—they stack so densely we barely recognize them, let alone name them. Practices like yoga and the Hoffman Process helped me peel back layers, but the silt ran deep. NSA was like clearing a dam, giving me a clean slate to start anew. Yet, without ongoing internal work, the silt would creep back. I learned this after the session, sitting alone, letting memories of Arjun surface. I named the grief, felt the ache, and let it move through me. No guide was needed—just presence. The weight lifted, and love returned—warmer hugs with my sons, deeper conversations.

This chapter's lesson is clear: we hold the power to heal. NSA, Reiki, or other practices can spark the release, especially when emotions are too tangled to face alone. But we can't rely on them forever. The danger lies in outsourcing our healing, waiting for a practitioner to fix us. The core work—identifying and releasing emotions—is ours. If we revert to old patterns, the silt rebuilds. But by embracing our emotions, we keep the river flowing, opening the way for joy, peace, and growth.

And yet, there is more. Releasing these emotions didn't just heal me—it opened the way for a new path to emerge. As I let go of the weight of grief and anger, I found myself stepping into a clearer, more aligned version of myself. It was as if the emotional silt had not only clogged my spirit but also obscured my purpose. With each release, I gained clarity, and with clarity came the quiet emergence of a higher manifestation of my true calling. By embracing higher emotions—love, acceptance, peace—I began to attract experiences and opportunities that resonated with this newfound energy. The process wasn't just about healing the past; it was about making space for the future—a future where my purpose feels more authentic, more expansive, guiding me toward a life that reflects who I am at my core.

12 Stages of Healing

From the book "The 12 Stages of Healing"by Dr. Donald M. Epstein, D.C.

12 **Community:** bring unique gifts to humanity; wholeness through shared presence

11 **Descent:** return renewed; love and serve through healed wounds.

10 **Ascent:** recognize you are intelligence itself; unite with universal flow.

09 **Light Beyond the Form:** sense energy within and around you; experience awe and joy.

08 **Emptiness in Connection:** embrace gratitude and vulnerability; trust and openness emerge.

07 **Resolution:** Release old patterns; experience peace and strength.

06 **Preparing for Resolution:** Gather energy and resources; prepare for transformation.

05 **Merging with the Stories:** See inherited stories; rewrite them to serve your higher self.

04 **Reclaiming Your Power:** Recognize where you gave power away; reclaim choice and possibility.

03 **Stuck in a Perspective:** The mind holds a fixed pattern; notice and connect with the stuck part.

02 **Polarity:** Blame or magical thinking; reconnect inner parts to access resources.

01 **Suffering & Disconnection:** Nothing works; connect to the body in helplessness.

Take Action: Building Emotional Awareness

Set Aside Time: Find 5–10 minutes daily, ideally in a quiet space.

Pause and Center: Sit comfortably, close your eyes, and take 5–10 deep breaths to settle your mind. Let your body relax, releasing any tension in your shoulders or jaw.

Identify and Name the Emotion: Ask, "What am I feeling right now?" Don't judge or rush. Emotions can be complex—anger might hide sadness, or joy might mingle with fear. Start with a broad label (e.g., "unsettled") and narrow it down (e.g., "anxious"). If you're unsure, explore physical sensations (e.g., "tight chest" might suggest anxiety). Use a feelings wheel or emotion list if needed, but aim to name it yourself over time.

Locate It in the Body: Scan your body from head to toe. Where does this emotion live? A lump in your throat? A flutter in your chest? A heaviness in your legs? Notice the sensation without trying to change it. Naming its location (e.g., "sadness in my throat") anchors it in your memory, making it easier to spot next time.

Reflect and Journal: Write down the emotion, its location, and any thoughts about why it's there (e.g., "Felt anxious in my stomach after a work call"). This builds a map of your emotional landscape. Over time, you'll notice patterns—maybe anger always tightens your jaw, or joy warms your chest.

Close with Gratitude: Thank yourself for showing up. Even naming one emotion is progress. End with a deep breath or a gentle stretch to transition back to your day.

Why It Matters: This practice builds emotional literacy, the foundation for releasing trapped energy. By naming emotions, you make them tangible, stripping away their power to overwhelm. Locating them in your body creates a bridge between mind and spirit, rooting your awareness in the present. Over weeks, you'll recognize emotions faster, even the subtle ones, preparing you for deeper work like releasing or replacing them, as outlined in the Take Action steps.

Tips:

Start small—5 minutes is enough. Consistency matters more than duration.

If emotions feel overwhelming, pause and breathe. You're not fixing them, just noticing.

Keep a journal to track progress. It's empowering to see how your awareness grows.

Be patient. Emotional recognition is a skill, and you're rewiring your brain with each practice.

This daily ritual is like learning to read the language of your soul. It's the first step to freeing your energy, setting the stage for the transformative work of letting go and rising higher.

For the full process, visit truenorthcoach.sg/resources

CHAPTER 7

STARS AND SIGNALS – ASTROLOGY'S ENERGY DANCE

In the Western world, astrology often gets a bad rap—and understandably so. Flip through a magazine or scroll online, and you'll find watered-down horoscopes promising love or luck based on your "star sign." "Aries, expect a fiery week!" Or "Pisces, romance is near!" It's vague, commercial fluff that reduces a complex system to a fortune-telling gimmick. Skeptics roll their eyes, and I don't blame them—I've been one. This shallow version of astrology fuels its reputation as pseudoscience, a parlour trick rather than a serious tool. But that's not the whole story. Astrology isn't an absolute truth handed down from the cosmos; it's a lens—a subjective, suggestive framework to explore the energy within and around us. It's not about predicting your future with certainty; it's about reflecting your unique way of being in a universe pulsing with possibility.

This shift in perspective about the value of astrology hit me after my self-healing work described in Chapter 6. Releasing grief's stuck energy through breathwork and Network Spinal left my body humming, lighter but restless. The journey so far had rewired me, I had learnt that energy is everywhere, emotions are its voice, and the body holds and releases it. Processing life's blows had tuned me to a higher frequency. Yet, a question gnawed at me: knowing we are all energy, part of the same vibrant pulse, wasn't enough. What was the nature of this energy? Could I truly sense its distinct currents—my own, those of others, the world's? To live with energy consciously, I needed to read its subtle language, to navigate its flow with intention. I yearned for a tool to interpret these invisible signals. Astrology slipped back into my life—not as a rigid rulebook I'd once rejected, but as a quiet guide, a tool I hadn't expected to embrace.

Like the Enneagram or Hawkins' scale, astrology offers a way to decode energy—not for everyone, but worth a look if we suspend judgment. It suggests we're all shaped by the same cosmic pulse, yet filtered through a unique blend of planets, signs, and houses at our birth. Are we all the same vibrating energy, as I've come to believe? Or does something make us distinct? Astrology says it's both: a universal hum, personalized by the stars.

My Winding Road with Astrology

My dance with astrology has been a tangle of curiosity, rejection, and rediscovery. As a teenager in India, I'd pore over "Linda Goodman's Love Signs" with friends, giggling as we paired Virgo with Leo or Pisces with Scorpio. It was a game, but it sparked wonder—could the stars really whisper who I was? That playful intrigue faded as I grew up. In India, astrology isn't child's play; it's a cultural cornerstone. Known as Vedic astrology or Jyotish, it's a meticulous system tied to the Vedas, charting the sky into twelve houses, each sliced into dashas (planetary periods) and bhavas (subdivisions) for granular detail. It can predict marriage, career, even misfortune with eerie precision. "Don't start a venture now; Saturn's in retrograde," an astrologer might warn, or "Jupiter's transit will bring prosperity—wait." It felt suffocating, a script I was expected to follow. Having shed Hinduism's rules, I tossed astrology aside as another confining leash.

But this journey through time has softened my skepticism. I'd felt energy move—chakra winds in meditation during the chakra-balancing workshop in Thailand, breathwork's rhythm, the release of tears in the Hoffman Process. I had felt emotions vibrating at varying frequencies on Hawkins' scale as my body responded on a chiropractor's table and through my daily practice of feeling and releasing emotions. If this shifting of energy was real, could the stars reflect it—not as a cage, but a mirror? That's when Steven Forrest's evolutionary astrology caught me. He didn't peddle fate; he offered a psychological tool. "Astrological knowledge coupled with an accurate birth chart is life's Rosetta Stone," he writes in "The Inner Sky." It decodes our energy—not to bind us, but to free us.

Astrology's Western Misadventure vs. Vedic Depth

Astrology's reputation in the West pales next to the view held by Vedic tradition. In the West, it's often a punchline—daily horoscopes in tabloids, oversimplified apps spitting out platitudes. It's a far cry from Jyotish's complexity, where astrologers calculate the course of planetary transits as they pass through decades, factoring in lunar mansions (nakshatras) and micro-periods. Vedic astrology sees the chart as a karmic blueprint, tracing past lives and future potentials. My family consulted astrologers who'd say, "Your Mars dasha brings conflict—avoid decisions." It's meaningful but rigid—too often a crutch to dodge accountability. Western astrology, in contrast, feels looser, especially in its pop form. But dig deeper, and you find voices like Forrest, who strips away fatalism for empowerment. Liz Greene, another luminary, brings Jungian depth, treating planets as archetypes—Mars as the warrior, Venus as the lover—mirroring our psyche. Robert Hand, a practical scholar, bridges tradition and modernity, urging us to use astrology for self-awareness, not escapism. These perspectives rescued astrology for me—not as a Western gimmick or Vedic dictate, but a tool to navigate my energy.

Life as a Story We Shape

What is life if not the story we tell ourselves? In the previous chapters we've peeled back layers—my roots, the numbing, the path to awakening, emotions, energy, release—to uncover truth. Now, we build that narrative. Why not craft one that lifts us, not drags us down? I've used many tools—the Enneagram, Graves' spiral, Hawkins' map—but my natal chart was the first. It's a treasure map, revealing the energies I carry and the paths they illuminate. It guided me from the ashes of the family business to coaching, a shift I only understood in hindsight through reading the stars.

We don't need to wait for pain—loss, failure, heartbreak—to reflect. Introspection can soften life's edges. Astrology doesn't guarantee control over external changes (though Hawkins suggests higher consciousness attracts better experiences). Even without that, it equips us to face what comes with greater clarity. The natal chart is a toolbox—showing why we act, feel, and falter, and pointing us forward.

A Mirror, Not a Mandate

I've always resisted boxes—family expectations, societal norms, systems claiming to define me. Vedic astrology's predictions felt like that: a prewritten play. Forrest flips it: "Astrology isn't about what happens to you—it's what you do with what happens." The natal chart—your sky at birth—isn't confining; it's freeing. No one dictates my path—I choose, using the stars as a guide.

Planetary placements suggest, not command. My Sun in Aquarius in the 6th house hints at a core tied to service and innovation—echoed in business and now coaching. My Moon in Sagittarius in the 3rd house craves emotional freedom and expression, a thread in my writing. My Virgo Ascendant projects practicality and precision. These are energies to wield, not rules to obey. Forrest calls it "a blueprint for your happiest path"—a nudge, not a noose.

Unlike Vedic fatalism, this approach empowers. In India, astrology's depth—houses split into sub-periods, planetary cycles tracked for years—can empower but also paralyze, depending on how it's used. I use my chart to reflect backward, learning from missteps, and forward, to set my course. It's a way-marker, not a wall.

What Is a Natal Chart? A Snapshot of the Sky

A natal chart, sometimes called a birth chart, is like a cosmic photograph. It is essentially a map of the sky as it appeared at the exact moment and location of your birth. Imagine the universe pausing for a split second when you took your first breath, with the Sun, Moon, planets, and stars all positioned in a specific arrangement above your birthplace. This circular diagram, divided into twelve sections, captures that unique configuration. It's not just a pretty picture; it's a symbolic representation of the energies present at your entry into the world. Astrologers believe these energies don't dictate your life but offer a starting point—a set of influences that shape how you experience and express the universal energy flowing through everything. Think of it as a personalized filter. The universe is buzzing with a vast, shared vibration—something we've explored in earlier chapters as the energy connecting all forms of life. The natal chart takes that universal hum and tunes it to your frequency, using the positions of celestial bodies to create a one-of-a-kind melody. To understand how this works, let's break it down into its key components: the signs, the planets (and other celestial bodies), and the houses.

The Signs: Cosmic Filters Made of Stars

The twelve zodiac signs—Aries, Taurus, Gemini, and so on—are the first layer of this filter. These signs are constellations, groups of stars that ancient cultures observed in the night sky and named to mark the Sun's yearly path (called the ecliptic). Each sign carries a distinct personality or flavour, colouring the energy of any planet or celestial body positioned within it. They're like lenses that refine the raw cosmic energy pouring into your chart, making it unique to you.

Here's how they group by element, which gives a sense of their vibe:

Fire Signs (Aries, Leo, Sagittarius): These are the spark plugs—bold, passionate, and action-driven. They bring heat and enthusiasm to whatever they touch.

Earth Signs (Taurus, Virgo, Capricorn): The grounded crew—practical, stable, and focused on the tangible. They anchor energy in the real world.

Air Signs (Gemini, Libra, Aquarius): The thinkers—intellectual, social, and communicative. They lift energy into ideas and connections.

Water Signs (Cancer, Scorpio, Pisces): The feelers—emotional, intuitive, and deep. They channel energy into the heart and soul.

When a planet lands in a sign, it takes on that sign's traits. For example, if your Sun (your core identity) is in Aquarius, an air sign, you might feel a pull toward independence and innovation. If your Moon (your emotions) is in Scorpio, a water sign, your inner world could be intense and private. The signs don't force you to be a certain way—they're the hues on your energetic palette, giving it a personal twist.

The Planets and Celestial Bodies: The Players on the Stage

Next up are the planets and celestial bodies—the Sun, Moon, Mercury, Venus, Mars, and beyond (in astrology, the Sun and

Moon are called "planets" for simplicity). These are the actors in your natal chart, each representing a different part of who you are. They're energy sources, and the signs they sit in determine how that energy shows up.

Here's a quick rundown of what the main players mean:

Sun: Your essence, the core of your identity—what lights you up and drives your purpose.

Moon: Your emotional self, your instincts, and the private you that not everyone sees.

Mercury: Your mind—how you think, communicate, and mentally process the world.

Venus: Love, beauty, and pleasure—what you value and how you connect romantically.

Mars: Your drive and ambition—how you assert yourself and chase what you want.

Jupiter: Growth and expansion—where you find luck and seek bigger horizons.

Saturn: Structure and discipline—where you face challenges and build resilience.

Uranus, Neptune, Pluto—the outer planets, tied to generational shifts. Uranus sparks change, Neptune fuels dreams, and Pluto transforms.

Each planet's energy gets filtered through its sign. Take Mars, the planet of action: in fiery Aries, it's direct and bold; in earthy

Capricorn, it's strategic and controlled. My Mars in Sagittarius, for instance, gives me a restless, adventurous push—always chasing the next big thing. The Sun, Moon, and planets don't act alone—they blend with their signs to create your unique energetic mix.

The Houses: Where Life Happens

Now, let's talk about the twelve houses—the stages on which these planetary actors perform. The natal chart is divided into these twelve segments, each representing a different area of your life. If the planets are the "what" and the signs are the "how," the houses are the "where." They show where your energy plays out, from your career to your relationships to your inner world.

Here's what each house covers:

1st House: Your self—identity, appearance, and how you show up in the world.

2nd House: Resources—money, possessions, and your sense of self-worth.

3rd House: Communication—thinking, talking, and connections with siblings and neighbors.

4th House: Home—family, roots, and your private foundation.

5th House: Creativity—romance, fun, and what you create (even kids!).

6th House: Work and health—daily routines, service, and taking care of yourself.

7th House: Partnerships—marriage, close relationships, and one-on-one bonds.

8th House: Transformation—intimacy, shared resources, and life's deeper mysteries.

9th House: Exploration—travel, philosophy, and the search for meaning.

10th House: Career—your public role, reputation, and ambitions.

11th House: Community—friends, groups, and your hopes for the future.

12th House: The subconscious—spirituality, dreams, and what's hidden.

The house a planet falls in shows where its energy takes root. My Sun in the 6th house ties my identity to work and service—I feel most myself when I'm helping others. My Moon in the 3rd house links my emotions to communication, so writing and talking soothe me. The houses give your chart context, turning abstract energies into real-life experiences.

Tying It All Together: Your Unique Energy Map

So, what does this all mean? The natal chart combines these elements—signs, planets, and houses—into a dynamic map of your energy. It's not a rulebook telling you what to do; it's a mirror reflecting who you are and where you might go. The snapshot of the sky at your birth sets the scene, the signs filter the energy through their starry personalities, the planets bring it all to life in your psyche, and the houses ground it in your everyday world.

For example, my Sun in Aquarius in the 6th house suggests a core self (Sun) that's inventive and free-spirited (Aquarius), focused on serving others (6th house). My Moon in Sagittarius in the 3rd house points to an emotional need (Moon) for truth and adventure (Sagittarius), expressed through words and ideas (3rd house). These pieces don't exist in isolation—they interact, creating a conversation of energies that's uniquely mine.

This isn't about fate locking you into predictable circumstances and experiences. The chart shows tendencies, not certainties—energies you can lean into or redirect. It's a tool to help understand yourself better, to see why you feel pulled in certain directions, allowing you to navigate life with a bit more clarity. For a beginner, it's a starting point: a way to dip your toes into astrology's waters and see what resonates.

Steven Forrest's evolutionary lens isn't the only way to interpret a birth chart. Liz Greene sees the chart as a psychological mirror—my Chiron in Pisces in the 7th house, she'd say, points to relational wounds I heal through empathy. Robert Hand grounds it practically: "Use the chart to act, not react." My Mars in Sagittarius in the 4th house—fiery home energy—explains past impulsiveness I now channel more productively. These voices enrich the toolbox, making astrology a dialogue, not a doctrine.

Understanding Your Natal Chart: The Nodes and Chiron's Dance

Astrology offers a map of our energy—a way to see the tendencies we carry and the lessons we're here to explore. The three points in the natal chart that I like to look at especially while trying to figure out my life purpose are the South Node, the North Node and the Chiron placements. The North and South Nodes are not physical planets but potent lunar nodes—mathematical points where the Moon's orbit crosses the Earth's path around the Sun. In Vedic astrology, they are known as Rahu (North Node) and Ketu (South Node), and they are considered Chayagrahas (shadow planets). They're cosmic markers of the soul's karmic journey, pulsing with the energy of destiny and release. They form the karmic axis in the circular birth chart, always opposite each other (e.g., Rahu in Aries, Ketu in Libra), shaping life's deepest lessons.

Ketu (south node) is the tail of the dragon in Vedic mythology, symbolizing past-life mastery and spiritual wisdom. It's the repository of what your soul has already learned—instinctive habits, talents, and attachments. Ketu's energy is inward, mystical, and detached, urging you to release outdated patterns. It can manifest as effortless skills (e.g., natural empathy in a nurturing sign) but also as stagnation if you cling to its comfort. Ketu asks, "What must you let go to grow?"

Rahu (north node), the dragon's head, embodies the soul's hunger for growth in this lifetime. It's a restless, magnetic force, pushing you toward uncharted desires and ambitions, like a storm tearing through a quiet village. Rahu's energy is worldly, intense, and sometimes obsessive, driving you to pursue goals that feel destined yet daunting (e.g., leadership in a bold sign).

It's the path of evolution, but its shadow can lead to illusion or overreach. Rahu asks, "What are you meant to become?"

Rahu and Ketu are among the most significant points in a Vedic chart, often outranking planets in karmic influence. They reveal the soul's evolutionary arc—Ketu's past shaping subconscious drives, Rahu's future guiding conscious aspirations. Their house and sign placements (e.g., Rahu in the 10th house for career ambition) pinpoint where growth and release are likely to occur. They also influence dashas (planetary periods), with Rahu or Ketu periods triggering intense transformation.

The third point, Chiron, does not find a place in Vedic astrology. In Western astrology, however, Chiron is known as the "wounded healer." This comet-like body, which orbits between Saturn and Uranus, was discovered in 1977. Named after the centaur in Greek mythology who was a healer despite his unhealable wound, Chiron represents our deepest pain, the wounds we carry, and the wisdom we gain by healing ourselves and others. It's a bridge between the material (Saturn) and spiritual (Uranus), blending vulnerability with transcendence.

Chiron points to a core wound in your life, often rooted in childhood or past experiences, that feels raw and unresolvable, like a crack in the soul's foundation. This wound shapes your struggles but also your gifts—by facing it, you develop empathy and the ability to guide others. For example, Chiron in Aries might indicate a wound around self-worth, leading to fierce independence but also a gift for empowering others. Its house and sign (e.g., Chiron in the 7th house for relationship wounds) show where pain and healing are prone to manifest. Chiron is a key player in modern psychological astrology, emphasizing self-awareness and healing. Its placement reveals where you face recurring challenges (e.g., rejection, abandonment) but also where you can transform pain into purpose. Astrologers use Chiron to explore trauma, resilience, and the hero's journey, making it central to personal growth charts. Its transits (e.g., Chiron return at age 50) mark healing milestones, prompting deep reflection.

In my natal chart, the South Node in Gemini in the 10th house and the North Node in Sagittarius in the 4th house form a polarity, two ends of a spectrum that shape my life's journey. Add Chiron in the 7th house, and you've got a dynamic trio that guides me through a dance of balance, growth, and healing. Let's break it down.

The South Node: Familiar Strengths

My South Node in Gemini in the 10th house points to energies that come naturally to me, especially in the early years of life. Gemini brings adaptability, curiosity, and a gift for communication, while the 10th house ties these to career, public roles, and reputation. Think of the influence of the South Node as a skill set you've mastered—whether from a past lifetime (as some astrologers suggest) or simply as a default mode you lean into. It's the ability to juggle ideas, connect with others, and thrive in visible, social spheres. This feels easy, like a well-worn path, so you might find yourself gravitating toward it often—leading projects, networking, or shaping how others see you, but here's the catch: what comes easy isn't always what pushes us forward. The South Node is comfortable, but it's not the whole story.

The North Node: The Stretch to Growth

Across the chart, my North Node in Sagittarius in the 4th house calls me to stretch beyond that comfort zone. Sagittarius craves wisdom, exploration, and truth, and the 4th house roots this in home, family, and inner emotional freedom. This is what I am destined to learn and experience in this lifetime—not a rigid fate, but a direction that calls and fulfills me. It's about nurturing myself and others, seeking deeper meaning, and building a foundation that reflects my authentic spirit. Unlike the South Node's outward buzz, this pulls me inward, asking for reflection and expansion.

Because these nodes are always opposites—in my case, Gemini and Sagittarius, 10th and 4th—moving toward the North Node requires effort. Learning anything new takes time and intention, like stretching a long-neglected muscle. The South Node's ease can make stagnation tempting, but the North Node invites growth through that necessary stretch.

Life as a Dance Between Poles

Here's the beauty: you don't abandon the South Node for the North. Life is a dance between these poles, a cycle that shifts every 18.5 years as the nodes change position in the sky. You move from South to North and back, refining both energies. The South Node's communication skills can serve the North Node's quest for wisdom—think teaching, storytelling, or creating a home that buzzes with ideas. The North Node's depth can temper the South Node's scattered tendencies, grounding a public role in purpose. This isn't about picking a side; it's about blending the best of both. Take Gemini's agility and pair it with Sagittarius' vision, balancing career with inner peace. Every cycle offers a chance to learn more, to weave these energies into a richer tapestry.

Chiron: The Alarm Clock and the Key

What happens when you resist this dance—when you cling to the South Node's ease and ignore the North Node's call? That's where Chiron steps in. In my chart, Chiron sits in the seventh house of relationships, highlighting where wounds show up—misunderstandings, disconnects, or betrayals. Chiron is an alarm clock. When life nudges you toward the North Node's growth—offering chances to nurture and explore—and you don't budge, Chiron rings out for attention. At first, it's a gentle nudge, a twinge in your partnerships. Ignore it, and it gets louder—relationship struggles that demand attention—until it kicks you out of bed, forcing you to face the lesson.

For me, this played out when I needed to shift toward my North Node's 4th-house call but didn't. The seventh house lit up with problems—maybe friction or emotional distance, initially in my marriage, signaling that it was time to move. But Chiron isn't just the wound; its symbol is a key for a reason. It unlocks treasures in your chart when you lean into its lesson. In my case, healing those seventh-house wounds revealed empathy—a gift for feeling and understanding others. This empathy strengthens my relationships, both personal and beyond, turning pain into a tool for connection.

Putting It Together

My chart tells a story of balance and growth:

South Node in Gemini, 10th House: I shine in communication and public roles—skills that feel second nature.

North Node in Sagittarius, 4th House: I am here to explore wisdom and nurture a soulful foundation—a stretch that rewards effort.

Chiron in the 7th House: Relationship wounds wake me up, but healing them unlocks empathy, enriching my dance between the nodes.

Life's cycles pull you between these poles, and Chiron ensures you don't sleep through the music. You don't ditch Gemini's chatter for Sagittarius' quest, for example; you blend them, letting empathy guide the steps. It's your dance—astrology just lights the floor.

Crafting a Story That Serves

Life's chaos becomes a story we shape. Astrology helps me write mine—not a dictated plot, but a personal tale. My Sun, Moon, and Nodes are characters; I choose their arcs in my story. Knowing Chiron heals through relationships, I lean into coaching's empathy. Seeing Mars' fire, I direct it with purpose. Forrest says, "Astrology poses questions, not answers." After my life's upheavals, it asked, "What does your North Node want to share?" The stars didn't explain loss—they reflected my shift to coaching. It's my story, guided by cosmic cues.

Skepticism and Subjectivity

Astrology isn't science—no data proves my Aquarius Sun drives service. I get the doubt around the usefulness of astrology; I lived through it. But truth isn't only lab-tested. Quantum physics suggests that observation shapes reality. If astrology helps me see myself, does it need a peer review? Forrest calls it "a language, not a law"—subjective, like art. Greene and Hand agree: it's a tool, not a tyrant. It's not for all, and that's fine. I ask for openness: test it as a guide, not gospel. It's one lens—beside Enneagram, Hawkins' scale—tuning to a soul's purpose.

Energy's Dance: Purpose Aligned

Astrology attunes me to my energy flow. My chart showed why I clung to the family business (South Node) and why it crumbled (North Node). Life nudged me toward coaching and sharing my journey; the stars echoed it. "The chart maps the soul's journey," Forrest writes. Pluto squaring my Sun wasn't doom—it was a call to align. My Sun pushes service but can detach. My Moon seeks freedom but can run wild. Knowing this, I adjust, crafting a story that fits.

Conclusion: A Tool, Not a Trap

Astrology's no cage—it's a mirror I've grown to trust. Forrest, Greene, and Hand make it a conversation, not a command. My chart maps energies to explore, not limits to obey. It's one lens among many, guiding me to my true self. In "Seat of the Soul," Gary Zukav says, "Authentic empowerment is the personality serving the soul's energy." Astrology aligns me there—not as superstition, but a signal. The stars light my way; I choose the steps.

Take Action: Feel Your Cosmic Pulse

Try astrology your way—deep or light.

Option 1: Chart it

Get your natal chart online (birth date, time, place). Spot your Sun, Moon, Ascendant. Not ready yet? Try Option 2 first.

Option 2: Reflect

Sun: What's your core trait? (e.g., bold, calm)

Moon: What's a private feeling? (e.g., yearning, peace)

Ascendant: How do others see you? (e.g., warm, sharp)

Breathe: Inhale 4, hold 4, exhale 6—five rounds. Where's the energy? Write it.

Ask: "What resonates for me?" Jot it down before sleep; revisit tomorrow.

No pressure. Whether charting or reflecting—you're affecting the trajectory of your story.

CHAPTER 8

THE BODY'S CODE – HUMAN DESIGN UNVEILED

Astrology in Chapter 7 flickered like a lighthouse beam, guiding me toward patterns I couldn't unsee. Life had already battered me with its heaviest storms: my son Arjun's death, a wound that never fully heals; the collapse of our family business; years of effort dissolving in a flash; my marriage fraying under the weight of grief and exhaustion. Chapter 6's breathwork and Donny Epstein's NetworkSpinal had started to unknot the tension coiled in my spine, releasing energy trapped in my body like steam escaping a pressure valve. Yet, even with that release, I couldn't settle. I had experienced a sense of calm like never before but I was still seeking answers. A question lingered, born from the Hindu philosophy woven into my upbringing: if spirituality lifts the soul as the eternal truth and casts the body as a fleeting illusion to transcend, what role does my body play? This skin, these bones, this racing pulse—I'm energy, yes, but I'm matter too, and it refused to be ignored.

Growing up, I had subconsciously absorbed the teachings of Hinduism. "You are not the body; you are the soul within." I had always assumed that this was a given for any spiritual seeker. But now, after feeling energy surge through my limbs during breath work, after sensing my gut whisper truths my mind couldn't grasp, it felt half-finished. Was my body just a cage to escape, or could it be a collaborator, a compass for this chaotic journey? That's when Human Design (HD) slipped into my awareness, not as a doctrine but as a map—not just of my soul, but of my body, murmuring, "This is your code, built for you alone."

I approached it with my usual skepticism. Another system? I'd spent decades peeling away rigid frameworks—Hindu rituals with their smoke and mantras, Vedic astrology's stern planetary dictates, even the Enneagram's tidy personality slots. HD didn't demand allegiance, though; it beckoned with a question: "What if your body knows something you don't?" That hooked me. It wasn't about faith—it was about exploration, and exploration is my lifeline to understanding. What I uncovered was a framework that didn't just nod to the cosmic threads of earlier chapters; it braided them into something I could feel in my hands, rooting my energy in my physical form.

A Brief History of Human Design: A Modern Mystic's Revelation

Human Design isn't an ancient relic unearthed from a forgotten shrine—it's a contemporary creation, birthed in 1987 by Ra Uru Hu, born Robert Allan Krakower, a Canadian physicist turned recluse. Ra wasn't your typical spiritual figurehead draped in robes; he was a man who'd walked away from a conventional life—physics labs, business suits, the grind of ambition—to drift into the wild edges of existence. By the mid-1980s, he'd landed on Ibiza, a sun-soaked Mediterranean island pulsing with a counterculture heartbeat. In the late '80s, Ibiza was a magnet for misfits—artists, hippies, seekers—its cliffs and turquoise waters a backdrop for those chasing something beyond the ordinary. There, over eight days, Ra claimed a "voice" delivered HD's framework: a fusion of astrology, the I Ching, the Hindu chakra system, Kabbalah's Tree of Life, and quantum physics. He dubbed it the "science of differentiation," a blueprint for how each of us is uniquely wired to navigate life.

I raised an eyebrow at first. A voice? It sounded like the opening of a sci-fi novel, not a credible origin story. But Ra's background in physics gave it a faint sheen of legitimacy, and his bold fusion of ancient wisdom with modern science hooked my interest. He wasn't selling enlightenment or rigid rules; he offered a tool to decode the energy that sets us apart. Ra spent the next 25 years refining and teaching HD until his death in 2011, leaving behind a system that's since spread through practitioners and seekers worldwide. I found it after Chapter 7's astrological tease, typing my birth details—into a free HD generator online. The chart that emerged wasn't just a pretty graphic; it was a jolt. It didn't stop at my personality or cosmic leanings—it drilled into my body, sketching how it's engineered to channel my energy. I leaned closer, tracing the lines, gates, and centers, sensing I'd stumbled onto something that could anchor my restlessness.

The Body: Hindrance or Vessel? A Paradigm Shift

Hindu philosophy had drilled a clear lesson into me: the body is transient, a distraction from the soul's timeless essence. Hindus believe the physical body is a temporary dwelling for the soul, a vessel that is subject to birth, growth, decay, and death. While the physical body will die, the soul is immortal and takes on a new physical form after death. Enlightenment meant detachment—meditation to quiet the mind, austerity to tame the flesh, willpower to rise above desire. I had always understood that to achieve spiritual growth, it's necessary to transcend the limitations of the physical body through practices like meditation, prayer, and focusing on higher values. I did not necessarily want to follow this path but I did accept the wisdom. Also after NetworkSpinal sessions left my spine tingling with released energy, after breathwork stirred instincts I couldn't name, that view cracked. My body wasn't silent—it was speaking, and I needed to listen.

Human Design turned my old narrative upside down. It didn't dismiss the body as a hurdle; it crowned it the vessel, custom-built to carry my unique energy into the world. That really struck me. In HD, the body isn't incidental—it's the foundation. HD borrows astrology to pinpoint your energy's flavour—that singular spark that's yours alone—and the I Ching to name its expressions through gates and lines. But its real magic lies in splitting your energy into two streams:

Design Energy: Locked in 88 days before birth, this (energy codes your DNA), it is your unconscious bedrock—your hardware. It's the instincts humming in your gut, the rhythms of your breath, the physicality you don't think about but live through, etched into your cells before you drew your first breath.

Conscious Energy: Captured at the moment of birth, this is your software—the personality you call "me." It's your thoughts, your emotions, the running commentary in your head that wrestles with decisions and dreams.

Both these energies dance in your HD chart or body graph, a diagram of how they align—or clash. The takeaway? My body isn't a random shell; it's a tailored container, designed down to its marrow for my soul's energy to flow through. We don't evolve by escaping the body—we evolve by embracing it, tuning it so energy moves unobstructed. This echoed Epstein's work from Chapter 6: emotions trapped in my shoulders, grief lodged in my chest, blocks my energy. HD went deeper: it's not just about clearing blockages—it's about syncing the body with its original blueprint, letting it hum as it was meant to.

Neutrinos: Cosmic Messengers with a Scientific Twist

HD ties this dual-energy imprint to neutrinos—elusive particles zipping from stars at near-light speed. First theorized in the 1930s by Wolfgang Pauli to explain missing energy in radioactive decay, neutrinos were detected in 1956, revealing them as the universe's second most abundant particles after photons. Born in stellar cores during fusion, they stream through space—and us—barely interacting with matter. About three trillion pass through every square inch of Earth each second, 70% from the Sun, 30% from distant constellations. Until 1998, science pegged them as massless, carrying no information. Ra Uru Hu begged to differ, claiming they imprint us with cosmic data at birth and 88 days prior.

Then came 1998: physicists at Japan's Super-Kamiokande observatory found neutrinos oscillate between types, proving they have a tiny mass—about one-millionth of an electron's. If they have mass, they could carry information, nudging Ra's theory into plausible territory. HD says neutrinos flood us constantly, and at key moments—birth and pre-birth—planets like Jupiter or Saturn act as lenses, focusing this stream to imprint our design and personality energies into our DNA. It's not fully proven, but it's not fantasy either: a universal energy field, filtered into unique human blueprints.

Picture it like a cosmic radio station. Stars broadcast a signal—neutrinos—carrying raw data. Planets tune the frequency: my Aquarius Sun means neutrinos hit me through Aquarius' lens at birth, infusing me with innovation and defiance. Pre-birth, my design energy set my body's tempo—a quieter, steadier beat. Ancient traditions named this prana or chi; HD calls it neutrinos, the "breath of stars," bridging science and spirit. It's poetic, sure, but grounded in a particle we've measured—a thread connecting my flesh to the cosmos.

Auras: Energetic Fingerprints

HD introduces auras as the core of how we engage with the world. Our aura is our energetic signature, a field that extends about two arm lengths around you, beyond our physical body and interacts constantly with the auras of others. Unlike personality traits, auras aren't about what we do but how our energy vibes with our environment and people. HD identifies five aura types, each with a distinct way of moving through the world:

Generators (Me): Enveloping, warm, magnetic. My Generator aura draws life toward me, like a steady orbit inviting opportunities to create and sustain. Near me, you might feel pulled in, warmed by my welcoming energy.

Manifestors: Repelling, bold, dynamic. Their aura carves out space for independent action, pushing others to keep up or step aside. It's a forceful, trailblazing energy.

Projectors: Penetrating, focused, insightful. Their aura dives deep, seeing into people and systems with laser-like clarity. They connect most powerfully when invited in.

Reflectors: Sampling, fluid, reflective. Their aura mirrors their surroundings, acting as a barometer for the collective energy around them.

Ra Uru Hu, the founder of HD, emphasized that auras don't limit what we can do—they reveal how we're wired to interact. Each type comes with a strategy, a practical tool to align with your aura's natural flow and reduce resistance:

Generators: Wait to respond. Let life bring options, then trust your gut's "yes" or "no." This keeps my energy magnetic, pulling in what lights me up.

Manifestors: Inform before acting. Give others a heads-up to smooth your impact, letting your bold energy flow without friction.

Projectors: Wait for invitations. Share your insight when welcomed, ensuring your penetrating aura lands with impact.

Reflectors: Wait a lunar cycle. Take time to let decisions settle, keeping your reflective aura clear and attuned.

These strategies aren't rigid rules but shortcuts to ease. When misaligned, we feel it: frustration, anger, bitterness, or disappointment. These emotions are our body's built-in detection system, signaling that our aura is out of sync. By following our strategy, we realign, letting our energy flow naturally. For me, waiting to respond feels like unclenching a fist—opportunities come, and my gut lights the way.

Beyond the Oversimplification

HD is often reduced to catchy slogans: "Manifestors manifest, Generators build, Projectors guide, Reflectors reflect." This oversimplification misses the mark, boxing each type into roles or implying limits on what we can do. I reject that—I refuse to be caged. Auras don't restrict potential; they shape how our energy engages the world to make things happen. A Generator like me can initiate, but pushing without a gut check drains me. A Manifestor can collaborate, but their aura thrives on bold, solo moves. Projectors can act without invitations, but their insight shines when welcomed. Reflectors can lead, but their strength lies in reflecting the collective's pulse.

The beauty of HD lies in its flexibility. It's not about what you can't do but about what fuels you. Each aura type can achieve anything—it's the approach that matters. My Generator aura pulls opportunities toward me when I respond, lighting me up. A Projector friend waits for my invite to share her wisdom, respecting my rhythm. This isn't limitation; it's harmony. Understanding others' auras fosters connection, letting us move together with less friction.

Conditioning: Auras and the distortion of our vessel

In Human Design, whether you're a magnetic Generator, a bold Manifestor, a guiding Projector, or a mirroring Reflector, your aura shapes how you connect with others. When someone steps into your 6–8-foot bubble—their aura mingles with yours, sparking influence. A Generator's warmth might pull you to overcommit, or a Manifestor's intensity might push you to conform, conditioning you to stray from your true self.

As children, we start as pure vessels, our unique energy flowing freely like water through an unkinked hose. But life, with its expectations and pressures, however bends us. Chapter 4's iceberg analogy showed how our personality forms, layered by conditioning from family, culture, and society. Chapter 6 explored Network Spinal Analysis and Donny Epstein's work, revealing how emotions lodge in our bodies, tightening muscles and shallowing breath. Human Design (HD) places a profound lens over this development process, focusing on how conditioning distorts our energetic flow and offering a path to deconditioning through the body itself. Unlike ancient spiritual traditions that urge us to transcend the body, HD positions it as the cornerstone of our journey, a vessel for our unique energy. Central to this is the concept of auras—our bodies' energetic fingerprints—and how they affect our interactions with the world and others.

In HD, conditioning is the process by which external influences—parents, teachers, society—twist our natural energy patterns, misaligning us from our innate design. This isn't just psychological; it's physical and energetic. When we're young, our open, malleable auras absorb the energies around us, adapting to fit expectations. A child whose design calls for patience might be pushed to act quickly, their body learning to override its natural rhythm. Over time, these adaptations become habits, etched into our cells, posture, and breath. My Generator aura, built to respond to life's cues, was conditioned to hustle like a Manifestor's—always pushing, initiating, forcing. The result? Tight shoulders, a racing heart, and a vague sense of being out of sync.

Conditioning doesn't just alter behavior; it disrupts the body's energy flow, creating resistance. HD teaches that this resistance manifests as specific emotions tied to our aura type: frustration for Generators, anger for Manifestors, bitterness for Projectors, and disappointment for Reflectors. These aren't random feelings but signals that our vessel is warped, our energy misaligned. For example, my constant frustration as a young adult wasn't just stress—it was my body signaling that I was overriding my design's need to wait and respond.

Deconditioning: Reclaiming Your Vibe

Conditioning warps our aura's natural flow, and deconditioning restores it. HD offers a path to decondition through the body itself. Unlike ancient spiritual traditions that urge us to transcend the body, HD positions it as the cornerstone of our journey, a vessel for our unique energy. By honoring your aura's unique flow—responding, informing, waiting, or reflecting—you can protect your energy. We decondition by following the strategy unique to our aura type. Growing up, I was pushed to hustle, my Generator aura twisted into forcing outcomes. My body bore the cost—chronic tension, shallow breath. Deconditioning is slow but tangible. By following my strategy—waiting to respond—I've begun to unravel those old patterns. My shoulders soften, my gut speaks clearer. Deconditioning, then, is about realigning with our aura's natural flow, peeling back layers of imposed habits. HD suggests this process takes seven years, tied to the body's cellular renewal cycle. As skin, bones, and organs refresh, we shed old patterns, letting our energy flow freely again. I'm partway through this journey—my gut's voice is louder, my urge to rush quieter. When I wait, life feels effortless. HD's seven-year timeline feels less like a deadline and more like a promise: as my body renews, so does my energy.

Here's how conditioning and deconditioning play out for each aura type:

Generators: Conditioned to initiate, we push and exhaust ourselves. Waiting to respond reconnects us to our magnetic flow, drawing in what's meant for us.

Manifestors: Conditioned to seek permission, they stifle their bold aura. Informing others before acting clears their path, restoring their trailblazing energy.

Projectors: Conditioned to overgive, they burn out without recognition. Waiting for invitations ensures their insight lands, recharging their penetrating aura.

Reflectors: Conditioned to rush, they lose their clarity. Taking a lunar cycle to decide keeps their sampling aura attuned, reflecting the collective with precision.

HD isn't a cage; it's a map. You can do anything—any type can—but some approaches fuel you, others drain you. Strategy is your guide to ease, not a boundary. By understanding your aura and deconditioning from what warps it, you reclaim your natural rhythm. For me, it's about trusting my gut and letting life flow.

Two Energies, Three Points: Ra Uru Hu's Cosmic Split

Ra's brilliance was splitting HD's design and conscious energies into three roles, distilled into a car analogy, revealing how they orchestrate our lives.

The Vehicle (Design Energy): Your body, the unconscious foundation—your hardware. It's the car itself, built to navigate life's road, instinctively knowing the route even if you don't.

The Passenger (Conscious Energy): Your personality, the conscious "you"—your software. It's in the back seat, observing the scenery, narrating the journey, but not driving.

The Magnetic Monopole (Driver): A mysterious force that steers, pulling your vehicle along your unique path, attracting circumstances and people that resonate with your energy. It's the driver, guiding you toward what's meant for you.

As we saw earlier, Ra's theory starts with two imprints: design energy (pre-birth) and conscious energy (birth). These split into three roles in practice. The vehicle—your body—is the unconscious design, wired to carry you through life. The passenger—your personality—rides along, experiencing it all. The magnetic monopole, a theoretical particle Ra adapted from physics, drives the show, drawing in experiences aligned with your energy. The goal? Be a good passenger—trust the vehicle and driver, and resist the urge to grab the wheel. The magnetic monopole is HD's wildcard. In physics, it's a hypothetical particle with a single magnetic pole; in HD, it's the driver, pulling your vehicle toward experiences that match your energy. As you decondition—clearing distortions—your frequency refines. The monopole then attracts higher-level circumstances, resonating with your rising consciousness.

This echoes Clare Graves' levels from Chapter 5: shed lower patterns (fear, force), and it draws in connection, clarity. Individual evolution lifts the collective, one ripple at a time. This also connects to earlier chapters. The Enneagram and astrology emphasize differentiation—we're all energy, expressed uniquely. HD adds the body: we're custom-built structures, designed to house this consciousness. Emotions (Chapters 4-5) are energy's language; when thwarted or not clearly expressed, they distort our physiology (Chapter 6). HD's car analogy frames it clearly: the vehicle runs smoothly when the passenger relaxes, letting the monopole steer. Conditioning—grabbing the wheel—throws the body out of alignment, mirroring the Enneagram's shadow patterns in a physical way. Life's goal? Be a good passenger—trust the vehicle and driver, don't wrestle the wheel. Conditioning is the passenger meddling; deconditioning is letting go, trusting the body's design.

Gates, Lines, and Channels: Decoding My Energy

Human Design (HD) offers a detailed map of your unique energetic blueprint, blending ancient wisdom from the I Ching, Kabbalah, astrology, and the chakra system into a visual tool called the BodyGraph. This chart reveals how your energy flows, interacts with the world, and shapes your experiences. At its heart are gates, lines, channels, and centers—components that work together to create a personalized energetic profile. Unlike broader systems like astrology or the Enneagram, HD's specificity lies in how these elements combine to show not just who you are but how your energy operates in real time. Below, we explore gates, channels, and the BodyGraph, explaining how they form and what they signify.

The BodyGraph: Your Energetic Blueprint

The BodyGraph is the visual core of HD, a diagram that synthesizes multiple systems into a single, cohesive map. It is generated using your birth data—date, time, and place—which determines how cosmic and personal energies imprint your design. It resembles a human figure with nine geometric shapes, called centers, connected by lines. These centers draw from the chakra system but are adapted in HD to represent hubs of energy processing, such as emotions, communication, or drive. Astrology provides the planetary positions, mapping them onto the 64 gates derived from the I Ching's hexagrams. Within each center are gates, numbered portals that carry specific energetic qualities. While the chakra system shapes the centers, Kabbalah's Tree of Life informs the energetic pathways. These pathways are called channels and they are the lines between the centers. Together, these elements form a dynamic picture of how your energy flows, where it's consistent, and where it's open to influence.

These inputs converge to create a snapshot of your conscious (personality) and unconscious (design) energies, calculated from your birth moment and three months prior, respectively. The result is a chart where colored (defined) areas show fixed traits, and white (undefined) areas indicate openness to external energies. This interplay reveals your unique way of navigating life.

Gates: Energetic Portals

Gates are the building blocks of the BodyGraph, 64 in total, each corresponding to one of the I Ching's hexagrams and mirroring the 64 codons of human DNA. Think of gates as energetic portals—specific frequencies you carry that shape how you experience and express life. Each gate has a distinct theme, like vision, desire, or imagination, influencing how you think, feel, or act. For example, Gate 41, tied to imagination and anticipation, might make you a visionary dreamer, while Gate 30, linked to desire and passion, could drive you toward intense experiences.

Gates appear in the BodyGraph's chakra inspired centers, either defined (colored) or undefined (white). Defined gates are consistent traits, like a steady signal you radiate. If Gate 41 (anticipation) is defined, you might naturally envision possibilities, radiating this hopeful energy to others. If Gate 30 (desire) is defined, you could exude a passionate drive that draws others in. Undefined gates, conversely, are where you're open, absorbing and amplifying the energies of those around you. With an undefined Gate 41, you might pick up others' dreams, inspiring you but not always anchoring your own. This openness isn't weakness—it's a space for growth and adaptability.

Each gate also carries a line, a number from 1 to 6, drawn from the I Ching's six-line hexagram structure. Lines add nuance, like a flavor to the gate's energy. Line 1 might ground a gate in practicality, while Line 5 could make it charismatic and influential. Together, gates and lines create a rich, layered picture of your energetic makeup.

Centers: Hubs of Energy

The nine centers in the BodyGraph are where energy pools and processes, similar to chakras but reinterpreted in HD as focal points for specific functions. Each center governs a different aspect of your experience, and whether it's defined or undefined shapes how you engage with that energy:

Root Center: Drive and adrenaline, the pressure to act or achieve.

Sacral Center: Life force, creativity, and stamina, the engine of vitality.

Solar Plexus Center: Emotions, desires, and passions, a wave of feeling.

Throat Center: Expression and communication, the voice of manifestation.

Heart Center: Willpower, ego, and self-worth, the push for impact.

Splenic Center: Intuition and survival instincts, a quiet inner knowing.

Ajna Center: Mental processing, analysis, and conceptualization.

Head Center: Inspiration and questions, the spark of big ideas.

G Center: Identity and direction, your sense of self and purpose.

Defined centers are consistent, like a reliable power source for that energy type. An undefined center, however, is receptive, taking in and amplifying the energies of others. For example, an undefined Solar Plexus might make you deeply empathetic but prone to absorbing others' emotions. Understanding your centers helps you navigate where you're fixed and where you're flexible.

Channels: Energetic Superhighways

When two defined gates in different centers connect, they form a channel—a vibrant pathway that links their energies into a cohesive theme. Channels are like superhighways in the BodyGraph, amplifying the traits of the gates they connect and creating a dynamic force in your design. There are 36 possible channels, each with a unique role, such as vision, connection, or passion. For instance, the Channel of Recognition (41-30), linking the Root's drive to the Solar Plexus's emotions, makes someone visionary and emotionally intense, driven to pursue what they imagine.

A defined channel activates both gates and their centers, creating a consistent energetic flow. If you have the Channel of Recognition (41-30), connecting the Root and Solar Plexus Centers, you might be fueled by a potent mix of imagination (Gate 41) and passionate desire (Gate 30), pushing you to chase big dreams with emotional depth. Undefined channels, like undefined gates, are open to influence, letting you experience those energies through others but not as a fixed trait. Channels add depth to your BodyGraph, showing how your energies combine to shape your interactions with the world.

How It All Works Together

The BodyGraph's power lies in its synthesis. The I Ching's gates provide specific energetic qualities, grounded in universal archetypes. The chakra-inspired centers organize these energies into functional hubs, while Kabbalah's pathways (channels) show how they connect. Astrology ties it to your birth, imprinting your conscious and unconscious energies. Together, they create a dynamic map: defined areas show your reliable strengths, undefined areas highlight your adaptability, and channels reveal how your energies flow as a whole.

Interpreting the BodyGraph is about seeing these parts as a system. For me, a defined Root Center and Gate 41 (anticipation) mean I'm driven to envision new possibilities, while Gate 30 (desire) in my Solar Plexus fuels my emotional intensity. The Channel of Recognition (41-30) ties my Root to my Solar Plexus, so when I lean into my visions, my passion amplifies, giving my pursuits a fiery edge. This interplay—gates, centers, channels—shows not just what I do but how my energy works best. It's a guide to flow, not a rulebook, helping me align with my natural rhythm.

Looking back, the Channel of Recognition mirrors my path:

Gate 41: The restless spark that propelled me into the business, hungry for new horizons.

Gate 30: The emotional teacher that showed me life has its own plan, guiding me to release expectations.

Line 6: In both gates, the observer's wisdom shines—my drive isn't impulsive, and my surrender isn't passive. They're refined by experience, shared as insight.

This isn't just a pattern—it's my story. I chased dreams because they called to me, something fresh and out of the ordinary. Gate 41's energy pushed me forward, but gate 30's fate forced me to adapt. In that surrender, I found clarity: my humanness—desiring deeply, stumbling, and rising—is a gift worth sharing. Through coaching and reflecting, I offer others the art of acceptance, the beauty of what is. Nothing captures my life more beautifully than this channel, this dance between restlessness and release.

For you, the Body Graph offers the same clarity. By understanding your gates, you see your core traits; your centers show where you're consistent or open; your channels reveal how your energies unite. Together, they form a map of your energy, showing you how to move through life with less resistance and more ease. It's not about limits—it's about unlocking the flow that's uniquely yours.

Incarnation Cross: Purpose in Focus

In Human Design (HD), the Incarnation Cross is a cornerstone of your energetic blueprint, illuminating the overarching theme of your life's purpose. It's not a rigid destiny but a guiding thread that weaves through your experiences, shaping how you move through the world and contribute to it. Derived from four key gates in your BodyGraph—two conscious (from your birth moment) and two unconscious (from three months prior)—the Incarnation Cross captures the essence of your unique role in the collective story. These gates, drawn from the I Ching's 64 hexagrams, sit at the Sun and Earth positions in your chart, anchoring your purpose in both your personality and your deeper, instinctive energy.

My Incarnation Cross is the Left Angle Cross of the Alpha 2, described as "seducing with dreams, waiting to lead others into the promised land." This resonates deeply with how I've lived. As a child, I'd gather my cousins on our veranda, spinning vivid tales of adventures we'd embark on, my words painting possibilities that lit up their eyes. That gift for weaving visions has carried through my life—whether pitching bold business ideas, writing this book to spark transformation, or coaching others to step into their potential. My cross reflects a purpose of inspiring through imagination, patiently waiting for the right moment to lead others toward something greater.

The Incarnation Cross doesn't dictate what you must do but highlights how your energy naturally flows to fulfill your purpose. It's like a melody that plays through your actions, relationships, and choices. For me, it's about crafting narratives that spark hope and possibility, then guiding others when the timing feels right. The Left Angle Cross of the Alpha 2 suggests I'm here to influence through personal connections, sharing dreams that invite others to follow—not by force, but by inspiration.

Your BodyGraph also reveals a vocation, a practical expression of your purpose in work or contribution. My vocation, "production scriptwriter," isn't about writing movie scripts but about crafting order from chaos—turning raw ideas into compelling narratives. This thread runs from my childhood storytelling to leading businesses, authoring this book, and coaching clients to build their own narratives while helping them to find clarity. Whether it's a business pitch or a coaching session, I'm shaping stories that move people forward.

The Incarnation Cross and vocation together offer a map, not a mandate. They show where your energy shines brightest, inviting you to lean into what feels most natural. For me, it's dreaming big, waiting for the right moment, and leading through stories that ignite possibility. Your cross, unique to your chart, holds a similar invitation—to discover the purpose that's been humming through your life all along.

The Math of Differentiation: HD's Unmatched Precision

What makes HD so uniquely personal? It's the sheer number of permutations. Astrology, with 12 signs and 10 planets, offers around 500,000 possible combinations. The Enneagram, with 9 types, wings, and instincts, provides a handful of variations. HD, however, is exponential:

64 gates, each with 6 possible lines (1 through 6), adding layers of nuance—like 64 musical notes, each playable in 6 octaves.

36 channels, pairing gates into specific energetic flows.

12 profiles (e.g., 6/3, 1/4), shaping your learning style and interactions.

768 variations of the 192 named incarnation crosses, defining your life's purpose.

Multiply these together, and HD yields over 2 billion unique charts. That's a system so precise it's almost like your fingerprint, dwarfing astrology's scope and the Enneagram's simplicity. This specificity is why HD feels like a tailor-made guide to your energy.

Why It Resonates: Evolution Through Form

HD says tune the vehicle, and energy flows—consciousness evolves. A warped vessel repeats loops; a clear one ascends. For me, it explained why pushing failed—my design is to wait. Now, I pause, feel my gut, act when it sings. Life responds—doors creak open, synchronicities bloom. It's not blind faith; it's mechanics I can test. My cross and gates hint at what's next—sharing, guiding—but I stay grounded, weighing it against reality.

Conclusion: The Body as Compass

HD reframed my body—not a prison, but a compass, built for my energy. Align it, and the soul shines. My cross, my gates—they're guides, not gospel. The noise quiets, the path sharpens. My body's wisdom leads—and I'm following. This isn't esoteric—it's your energy, practical and real. Start here, stay curious. It leads into Chapter 10's Gene Keys.

Take Action: Explore Your Incarnation Cross

HD can feel overwhelming—charts, gates, lines—but it's a tool, not a puzzle. Let's ground it with your incarnation cross, your energy's arc.

Get Your Chart: Use a free HD generator online (enter birth date, time, place).

Find Your Cross: Check the "Incarnation Cross" section—usually named (e.g., "Left Angle Cross of the Alpha 2"). It's based on your conscious and unconscious Sun and Earth gates (top four numbers in black and red columns).

Read Its Theme: Search your cross's name online (e.g., "Left Angle Cross of the Alpha meaning"). It's a glimpse of your energy's purpose—like mine, blending vision with timely leadership.

Reflect: Recall a moment you lived it. For me, it was advising my friend—vision met timing. When did your cross come alive?

Act Small: Set one intention based on it.

Mine: "Today, I'll share one idea when it feels right."

Try it—see what shifts.

CHAPTER 9

POETIC PULSE – GENE KEYS AND THE GOLDEN PATH

When I first encountered Gene Keys, I didn't expect it to hit me the way it did. I'd spent years wrestling with life's big questions—purpose, meaning, how to live well—often through a lens of logic and skepticism honed by running a family business. Systems like Human Design had already given me a practical map of my energy, showing me how I'm wired to move through the world. That map tightened my grip on a truth: my form isn't random; it's built for my energy. Yet, as I traced its lines, a question pulsed louder: What's this energy for? Not just how it moves, but what it means—what it sings. Then came Gene Keys, slipping in like a friend's murmur over coffee, saying, "Here's the beauty in your mess."

Gene Keys? - It was different. It didn't demand I make sense of it. I'd read Richard Rudd's words, and instead of analyzing them, I felt them seep into me—like poetry that didn't need decoding, ancient wisdom that landed in my bones without effort. Yet, for the logical seeker in me, it offered something more: a structured path to explore that wisdom, a way to bridge doing and being. This chapter is about that journey—not mine alone, but one you can take too. We'll unpack Gene Keys, dive deep into its Golden Path, and explore how it works as both a poetic gift and a practical guide. My story will wait until the end, briefly, to show how it ties in—not as the focus, but as an example. This is about the system itself yet meandering through the poetry of Gene Keys, to give you every angle I've come to cherish.

I was no pushover for airy ideas thanks to my logical mind, honed by years in the family business, I used to scoff at anything unprovable. But this edge had already been softened, I am no longer a skeptic but a logical seeker. As a Generator, Human Design showed me a mechanical truth: my sacral engine is designed to respond powerfully to life's prompts, rather than to initiate from a place of uncertainty. It's a yang system—structured, precise, a guide to how my body and consciousness interplay. It reveals my Generator type, guiding me to operate by waiting for life's invitations, responding with my sacral energy, and resting when needed. Practical, yes, but it left me wondering about the why—the deeper song beneath the mechanics. And that's when Gene Keys answered my call. It wasn't about rules or proof; it was a quiet invitation to reflect, to see myself anew. Human Design mapped my form; Gene Keys sang its essence—a duet that felt right.

This chapter shifts from form to meaning, building on the roots, cracks, healing, signals, and blueprint of earlier chapters, now humming a new verse. Gene Keys and Human Design share the same roots yet they are different. Gene Keys' essence is its DNA coding, emotional frequencies, and the Golden Path's transformative sequences. Gene Keys uniqueness is also its focus on contemplation as a practice. Not unlike Hinduism's most revered text, the Bhagavad Gita, I consider Gene Keys a wisdom that speaks to the moment.

How Gene Keys Differs from Human Design—and Where They Align

Human Design (HD) and Gene Keys share a skeleton but wear different skins. They are two interconnected systems that offer insights into personal growth and self-awareness, both rooted in the 64 hexagrams of the I Ching, ancient archetypes tied in the Gene Keys system, to planetary placements at birth. The "gates" in Human Design and the "Gene Keys" in the Gene Keys system refer to these same 64 archetypes, but they differ in their focus, application, and interpretation. These 64 archetypes are calculated using your birth date, time, and location, and they appear as specific "activations" in your chart or profile. For example:

- In Human Design, your chart (called a Bodygraph) shows gates activated by planetary positions, such as your Conscious Sun or Unconscious Mars.

- In Gene Keys, your Hologenetic Profile maps the same numbers (e.g., Gene Key 28 corresponds to Gate 28) to archetypal patterns for personal transformation, with sequences like Activation, Venus, and Pearl guiding deeper contemplation.

Gene Keys: Poetry Meets Purpose

Gene Keys, created by Richard Rudd, is a contemplative system that blends the I Ching's 64 hexagrams, astrology, genetics, and spiritual traditions into something unique. It builds on the same framework as Human Design—both use the same 64 gates, tied to planetary positions at birth—but where Human Design maps how your energy functions, Gene Keys asks what this energy feels like and what it's becoming. Human Design is a blueprint of mechanics: it tells you your type (say, a Generator), your authority (how you decide), your centers (where energy flows or doesn't). Gene Keys takes those same gates and turns them into emotional frequencies, coded in your DNA, waiting to be explored.

Richard Rudd, was a student of Ra Uru Hu, the founder of Human Design. Rudd built Gene Keys on the structural framework of Human Design's gates, so the numerical correspondence is identical—Gate 1 is Gene Key 1, Gate 2 is Gene Key 2, and so on. Both systems use these 64 energies to reveal aspects of your personality, purpose, and potential, making them inherently related.

While they share this foundation, Human Design gates and Gene Keys diverge in their purpose, presentation, and practical use. The main point of difference between the two systems is on their focus and purpose. Human Design Gates are part of a detailed, mechanical system—the Bodygraph—that maps how your energy functions in the world. Each gate represents a specific trait or energy (e.g., Gate 1 is "Creativity," Gate 28 is "Struggle") and connects to centers (like the Throat or Root) via channels. The focus is practical: how you operate, make decisions, and interact with others based on your "Type" (e.g., Generator, Projector), "Strategy" and "Authority".

Gene Keys on the other hand, takes a contemplative, transformative approach. Each Gene Key is a journey through three frequency levels—Shadow (challenge), Gift (potential), and Siddhi (highest expression)—each, for the 64 energies (e.g., Gene Key 1 moves from "Entropy" to "Freshness" to "Beauty"). The focus is introspective: unlocking your highest potential and evolving consciousness through reflection. For example, Gate 41 in Human Design is about imagination and initiating new experiences, tied to the Root Center. Gene Key 41 explores the Shadow of "Fantasy," the Gift of "Anticipation," and the Siddhi of "Emanation," encouraging you to contemplate how fantasy can transform into purposeful vision.

They also differ in the way they are structured and how they can be applied. HD Gates are fixed components of a larger system. They're activated (defined) or dormant (undefined) in your chart, influencing how energy flows between centers. For instance, if Gate 20 (the "Now") connects to Gate 57 via a channel, you have the "Channel of the Brainwave," amplifying intuition. Human Design provides a "user manual" with specific guidance—e.g., Generators respond, Projectors wait for invitations—based on these connections. Gene Keys are organized into sequences (Activation, Venus, Pearl) that guide you through a personal narrative. You don't just have a map; you're invited to explore each Gene Key deeply, often through contemplation or journaling, to shift from Shadow to Gift. There's no rigid "strategy" like in Human Design—just an open-ended process of self-discovery.

As an example, in Human Design, Gate 10 (Self-Love) in the G Center might show how you express authenticity, especially if it forms the 10-20 Channel of Awakening. In Gene Keys, Gene Key 10's journey from "Self-Obsession" to "Naturalness" to "Being" asks you to reflect on how self-focus can evolve into effortless presence.

But where both systems really stand apart is in their language and tone. In HD, the language is technical and grounded, often using terms like "pressure," "expression," or "correction" to describe gate energies. It's about mechanics—how the gate fits into your design and influences behavior. For instance, Gate 62 is "Details," emphasizing precision in communication. Whereas in Gene Keys, the language is poetic and metaphysical, framing each key as a spectrum of consciousness. Gene Key 62 moves from "Imprecision" (Shadow) to "Precision" (Gift) to "Impeccability" (Siddhi), inviting a deeper, emotional resonance with the energy.

HD Gates offer a snapshot of your traits within a broader system. They're one piece of the puzzle—your full design (Type, Authority, Centers) shapes how each gate manifests. A single gate's meaning is contextual, not standalone. But each Gene Key is a complete story. The Shadow-Gift-Siddhi framework gives you a layered, universal exploration of that energy, applicable beyond your chart. It's less about your "wiring" and more about universal human potential. Consider Gate 15 in Human Design, which is "Extremes," tied to loving humanity's diversity in the G Center. Gene Key 15 spans "Dullness" (Shadow) to "Magnetism" (Gift) to "Florescence" (Siddhi), broadening the theme into a personal and spiritual evolution.

Human Design and Gene Keys may be different yet they complement each other. They are like two sides of the same coin: one practical, one philosophical. They relate because they start with the same 64 energies, but they serve different needs:

Human Design gives you the "what" and "how"—a blueprint of your energetic mechanics and actionable steps to live in alignment (e.g., "Wait to respond" for Generators).

Gene Keys provides the "why" and "where to"—a deeper dive into the meaning behind those energies and a path to transcend limitations through contemplation.

For instance, if your Human Design chart shows Gate 28 defined, you might learn it's about resilience through struggle and how it connects to your Spleen Center for survival instincts. Exploring Gene Key 28, you'd contemplate moving from "Purposelessness" to "Totality" to "Immortality," adding a transformative layer to that resilience. While Human Design focuses on behavior and decision-making; Gene Keys focuses on consciousness and growth, HD Gates are part of a fixed chart; Gene Keys are a fluid journey through sequences. Human Design shows you how you're wired; Gene Keys helps you evolve what's within that wiring. In short, gates tell you what you're working with, while Gene Keys guide you to refine it into something extraordinary. You can use Human Design to navigate daily life and Gene Keys to explore your soul's potential—together, they're a powerful duo for self-understanding.

Beyond Mechanics: The Emotional Core

The Gene Key system stands apart from HD through its unique foundation in DNA coding, linking each of the 64 Gene Keys to specific amino acids. HD nods to biology but stays surface-level. Gene Keys dives deep, proposing each gate aligns with a DNA codon (e.g., Gate 41 to methionine, Gate 31 to leucine). The chemical code contained within the DNA, although locked in from birth, is highly sensitive to vibrating energy.

Each Gene Key (gate) holds three states, reflecting emotional frequencies:

Shadow: A low-frequency emotion—like fear, anger, or doubt—that clouds your energy—energy stuck or misdirected.

Gift: A creative, balanced state—like courage, patience, or clarity—that emerges when you face the Shadow—energy flowing freely.

Siddhi: A transcendent, almost saint-like vibration—like love, peace, or unity—that hints at your highest potential-energy at its peak.

These aren't steps but vibrations of the same essence. Take Gate 41: its Shadow is Fantasy (restless dreaming), its Gift is Anticipation (patient possibility), its Siddhi is Emanation (pure creative flow). Same root emotion—hope, perhaps—shifting from low to high frequency. Gene Keys suggests Shadows drag us down, Gifts lift us, and Siddhis soar.

Rudd ties this to DNA, suggesting each gate aligns with one of the 64 codons in our genetic code—biological building blocks that might hum these frequencies too. This connection suggests a profound idea: if our emotions are fundamentally a blend of chemical reactions in the body, then the three states of each Gene Key - Shadow, Gift and Sidhi - could represent distinct expressions of a single emotional energy. The Shadow might reflect a lower frequency expression, the Gift a balanced and creative one, the Sidhi, its highest most transcendent form. This echoes David Hawkins' Power vs. Force, where emotions like fear (low), vibrating at lower frequencies rise to courage (mid-range) and love (high) vibrating at higher ones This also aligns beautifully with Clare Graves Map of conciousness, where shifting to higher frequencies corresponds to an evolution in consciousness. Through this lens, the Gene Keys not only map each key to a core emotion but also reveal its spectrum of expression - from limitation to liberation. Beyond mere analysis, the poetic brilliance of Gene Keys lies in its vision of the Sidhi, offering a glimpse of the sublime potential awaiting us when we unlock these higher states.

Rudd suggests contemplating the gene keys shifts our cellular resonance—a poetic leap beyond HD's scope. For example, Gate 41 aligns with methionine, sparking protein synthesis; Gate 31 with leucine, shaping structure. Rudd posits that contemplating a gene key's states—say, moving from Fantasy to Anticipation—rewires its codon's expression, shifting our emotional and physical being. Science may squint at this, but I feel it. Sitting with Gene Key 41, my restless chasing quiets into a patient pulse—a cellular shift I can't prove but can't deny.

A Daily Wisdom Guide: The Bhagavad Gita Parallel

In India, there's a practice of opening the Bhagavad Gita, which is the most revered Hindu text, randomly to any page for a wisdom nugget to guide the day. The Gita brims with insight—every line a deep message, tailored to the moment by some unseen grace. Gene Keys mirrors this. With 64 Gene Keys, each layered with Shadow, Gift, and Siddhi, it's a living oracle. Pick a Gene Key—say, Gene Key 10 (Self-Obsession to Naturalness to Being)—and read a page from Rudd's Gene Keys book. The Shadow might reveal where you're stuck; the Gift, a way forward; the Siddhi, a glimpse of your highest potential. Like the Gita, it's brimming with wisdom, adaptable to any day's need.

I've tried this many times. The Shadow spoke to my trapped feeling; the Gift offered a path to alchemize it; the Siddhi hinted at a peace beyond. It wasn't random—it was medicine. Gene Keys, like the Gita, invites this daily dance with wisdom, contemplation as the key to unlock its depth.

Meditation, Concentration, and Contemplation: Rudd's Paths

What I found particularly fascinating was Rudd's take on spiritual practice. He outlines three paths:

Meditation (Yin Path): This is the right-brain approach—holistic, not reductionist. It's about emptying the mind, transcending thought, a path of effortlessness. I've tried it, but my restless mind never settled there.

Concentration (Yang Path): The opposite end, rooted in the left brain's logical questing. It's effort, focus—the path of yoga, whether karma, bhakti, or mantra—all moving toward truth. It's disciplined, but too rigid for me.

Contemplation (Taoist Way): The middle path, nebulous unless you get it right. It's less extreme, suited to everyday life. It doesn't push hard in any direction—it's gentle, playful, presupposing breakthroughs come in relaxation, not force.

I love this because I've always known meditation alone isn't my path—I need my brain engaged, but not so much that it turns into the grind of concentration. Contemplation is my sweet spot. It's a search, like the Buddha's middle way, but not intense—just a playful appreciation of mystery, content to enjoy the journey as much as the breakthroughs. The key? Having an object to contemplate. That's what Gene Keys is designed for—each key a theme to hold lightly, letting insight bloom in its own time. I'll sit with 41's anticipation: What does it mean to wait without grasping? Over time, it shifts from a question to a feeling, a quiet alignment in my chest.

How to Contemplate

Pick a gene key - say, Gene Key 10 (Self-Obsession to Naturalness to Being). Read the Shadow—where do you fixate? Feel it—tightness, chatter. Then the Gift—Naturalness—when have you felt ease? Imagine it growing. The Siddhi—Being—what's it like to just be? Sit with it—5 minutes, an hour, daily. Journal or wander. The Shadow softens; the Gift roots. Rudd says it shifts DNA, but even without that, it shifts you. This pausing practice—stopping briefly to attune to life's wisdom—rewires your DNA, sending higher-frequency signals that trigger endorphins and open your heart. Each pause builds trust in your inner light, aligning you with your potential.

The Golden Path: Three Sequences to Transcendence

The Golden Path is the heart of Gene Keys—a three-part journey through your Hologenetic Profile, a chart derived from your birth data. "Hologenetic" reflects a unified field, like DNA, encoding your full potential across layered energies. These energies coil into your being through gestation (three 3-month cycles) and three, 7-year cycles: physical (0-7 years), emotional (7-14 years), and mental (14-21 years). Conditioning may lock these energies in Shadow frequencies, but the Golden Path uncoils them, starting from the outer mental layer back to the innermost prenatal core. It's not about fixing you; it's about uncovering your essence through contemplation. Richard Rudd sees the Gene Keys not as fixed traits but as a code, like a combination lock, unlocked through sequences—Activation, Venus, and Pearl. While Rudd suggests a 7-year cycle for transformation, it's a spiral, not a race, and non-linear: you can contemplate any Gene Key that calls to you or follow the sequences for structured "uncoiling." Each sequence tackles a core question, guiding you from Shadow to Gift, and perhaps to Siddhi, with practical steps to embody the change.

Activation Sequence: Grounding in Purpose

What It Asks: What am I here to do?

The Activation Sequence, the first phase, focuses on your four Prime Gifts. The four key gates - Life's Work, Evolution, Radiance, and Purpose - form your "Genius". These are your Sun and Earth placements at birth and around 88 days before, locking in your core essence. In Human Design these four coordinates are defined as your prime gifts and they help to determine your incarnation cross. The corresponding Gene Keys in your profile, reveal your core strengths and challenges. This phase is about grounding, anchoring you in your unique purpose by confronting Shadow patterns like fear, resistance, or self-doubt.

The Sphere of Life's Work

What It Is: Life's Work is tied to your Design Sun gate, which comes from the position of the Sun at the moment of your birth in your birth chart. This is where your deeper purpose meets the outside world. It reflects what you are here to embody and share with the world. This is your external expression—the quality or gift you naturally radiate outward. It's about your mission or the role you play in life, often visible in your work, creative output, or how you engage with others. The shadow in this Gene Key will show you the patterns in your nature that prevents you from finding the kind of role that perfectly suits you.

If your Life's Work is Gate 47 (Oppression to Transmutation to Transfiguration), you might be here to embody the gift of transmutation. This could mean turning challenges or confusion into wisdom and sharing that transformative process with others—perhaps as a teacher, guide, or inspirer.

The Sphere of Evolution

What It Is: Linked to your Design Earth position, this gate reflects the lessons and growth you're meant to experience in life. Whereas your life's work is the expression of what you do, your Evolution is the turbine that drives what you do. It's your internal challenge—a recurring theme or obstacle you're here to work through and refine over time. It drives your personal evolution, often through struggles or breakthroughs that teach you resilience and wisdom. More internal—this is felt in your private journey rather than being outwardly obvious to others.

The Sphere of Radiance

What It Is: Connected to your Personality Sun position, this gate shows how your vitality and energy shine out into the world. It's your energetic glow, in other words, your aura—the way your presence uplifts or influences others, enhancing your Life's Work. It adds charisma, warmth, or magnetism to how you express your gifts, amplifying both your impact and your joy. Very noticeable—others feel this in how you light up a space or inspire them.

The Sphere of Purpose

What It Is: Purpose is tied to your Unconscious Earth gate, derived from the position of the Earth 88 days before your birth. Purpose here is not about what we are here to do but about the quality of our consciousness. It represents your internal foundation, the essence that grounds and sustains you from within. This is your inward-facing essence—what keeps you centered, nourishes your soul, and gives your life meaning on a personal level. It often operates subtly or unconsciously, acting as your inner anchor. Your purpose is designed to be unlocked by Life.

This sequence is about building a foundation. You observe Shadows without judgment, letting contemplation rewire your responses. Over time, you feel more grounded, with less tension, as your actions align with your purpose. For me, this meant trusting my role as a storyteller and coach, crafting narratives that inspire, as seen in writing this book.

Venus Sequence: Healing Your Relationships

What It Asks: How fulfilling are my connections—with myself, others, life?

The Venus Sequence explores your emotional journey and relationships. It includes six gates that map your heart's path, from your Purpose to your deepest Core Wound, guiding you toward greater love and connection, while diving into your relationships and uncovering ancestral patterns. These six spheres flow from Purpose (from the Activation sequence) through Attraction, IQ, EQ, SQ, to your Core Wound. This emotionally intense sequence unearths childhood conditioning and defensive habits.

Sphere of Purpose

What It Is: Carried over from the Activation Sequence (Personality Earth), but here this gate anchors your emotional life. This Gene Key grounds the sequence. It's the stable base for how you approach love, relationships, and self-connection. It sets the tone for your emotional world, offering a foundation for how you relate to others and yourself. It is about what draws you to others, often unconsciously.

Sphere of Attraction

What it is: In Human Design, the Moon represents emotional needs, instincts, and subconscious drives. Connected to the unconscious moon placement this gate reflects deeper, less conscious emotional patterns that influence how you process and express emotions. It acts as the subconscious source of your emotional energy, reflecting how you instinctively feel and seek security. It's the "raw" emotional undercurrent that influences your inner world.

Sphere of EQ

What It Is: Connected to your conscious Moon position, this gate shows how you feel and express emotions in relationships. It's your emotional flow—the way you experience and share your heart, whether openly or guarded. It defines your emotional availability and vulnerability, influencing how deeply you connect. It's about deliberate emotional sharing and vulnerability.

Sphere of IQ

What It Is: Linked to your conscious Venus position, this gate reveals your mental patterns in relationships—how your mind processes love, attraction, and connection. It's the lens through which you think about relating, shaping conscious defenses (like overanalyzing partners) or clarity (aligning thoughts with your heart). It influences how you mentally navigate relationships, guiding you toward emotional wisdom. It's about mental clarity or blocks in love.

Sphere of SQ

What It Is: Linked to your unconscious Venus position, this gate reflects your spiritual quotient, the measure of your ability to remain connected to the spiritual heart of life. It reveals subconscious patterns of how you open to universal love, rooted in early childhood and ancestral imprints. It guides your soul to grow, connect, and find meaning through others, fostering transformative, soulful bonds. It's about unlocking the floodgates of love within you. It involves the triggering of a pre-coded awakening sequence that begins before we are born.

Sphere of Core Wound

What It Is: Tied to your unconscious Mars position, this gate reveals your deepest emotional hurt or vulnerability. It is the nexus of the sacred wound that you carry in this life and this wound connects you to all other human beings. It's your primary challenge in expressing your unique energy through love and relationships—a subconscious block that holds the key to profound healing. By facing this wound, you transform pain into wisdom and compassion, unlocking authentic emotional connection. It's about your deepest hurt and how to heal it to live fully as you.

This sequence releases emotional barriers, fostering self-love and authentic connections. Contemplation—meditating, journaling, pausing when triggered—surfaces memories, like my childhood moments of feeling unseen in a bustling Indian family. Physically, you might notice lighter shoulders or deeper breaths as emotions release. Emotionally, you grow resilient, meeting triggers with curiosity, deepening your relationships.

Pearl Sequence: Integrating with the World

What It Asks: How do I contribute and prosper in community?

The Pearl Sequence reveals how you prosper by being yourself and contributing to the world. It includes four gates that guide your integration into the collective and your path to abundance. The four gates—Vocation, Culture, Brand and Pearl—reveal your "Prosperity," abundance through authenticity.

Sphere of Vocation

What It Is: We begin our journey here with the Sphere of your Core Wound which now becomes the Sphere of your Vocation. This gate reflects your unique calling or path of growth. It's your true work—where your energy feels most alive and aligned with your potential. It's the intersection of your talents and the world's needs, often unfolding as you mature. It's your calling—where energy thrives. The question this sphere asks is: how can I be of the utmost service to the world in the short time that I am alive?

Sphere of Culture

What It Is: Connected to your Unconscious Jupiter position, this gate shows how you connect to the collective. It's your bridge to community—how you fit into or shape group dynamics and societal structures. It guides how you contribute to the larger whole, influencing culture or collaboration. It's your bridge to the collective.

Sphere of your Brand

What it is: This is the sphere of our Life's Work from the activation sequence but here it is viewed through a different lens. Your Brand is the extension of your personality, your outer representation in life. Your brand is like a homing beacon and when you have the courage and take the initiative to wield your own Brand - your highest truth - then you will draw your true allies into your life.

Sphere of Pearl

What It Is: Tied to your Conscious Jupiter position, this gate represents the reward of living authentically. It's your prosperity—not just material wealth, but the ease, grace, and abundance of being yourself. It blooms when you stop striving and start embodying your truth, offering a natural flow of rewards. It's the reward—ease, being yourself fully.

This sequence brings mental clarity and practical shifts. You might redefine success or shift careers, as I did by prioritizing coaching over endless hustling. Contemplation becomes a way of life, like pausing to notice a bird or a breath, anchoring presence. Physically, your body feels vibrant; mentally, limiting beliefs dissolve, letting your presence ripple outward through service.

The 7-Year Spiral: A Cycle of Renewal

Rudd frames the Golden Path as a 7-year spiral, a transformative cycle tied to the body's cellular renewal, where cells—skin, bones, organs—refresh every seven years. This biological rhythm mirrors a spiritual rebirth, allowing you to shed conditioned patterns and embody your true essence. The spiral is flexible—some move faster, others linger—guided by your commitment to contemplation. For me, Gene Key 5's call to Timelessness resonates here, reminding me to trust the journey's natural rhythm rather than rush toward change.

The 7-year cycle's significance spans science and mysticism. Biologically, cellular renewal embeds new energetic patterns as old habits dissolve. Spiritually, seven is sacred—seven chakras, seven days of creation, seven-year astrological cycles—symbolizing completion and transformation. Rudd describes this as a journey of embodiment, where contemplation shifts you from Shadow to Gift, with Siddhis hinting at your highest potential. The spiral is not a one-time journey but a lifelong practice, each cycle deepening your alignment with your design.

The 7-year spiral is a shift from fragmentation to wholeness. Shadows fade as you embrace them with compassion. Gifts become your default, shaping your actions. Siddhis offer glimpses of unity, like moments of flow when coaching or writing. Physically, tension releases, your body feeling lighter. Emotionally, you meet triggers with grace, as I did when moving from rejection fears to openness. Mentally, clarity emerges as beliefs about worth or success dissolve. Socially, your presence inspires, deepening connections. The 7-year spiral is both personal and collective. Rudd speaks of a "Great Change," a global shift toward higher consciousness, where individual contemplation fuels humanity's evolution. My Gene Key 63, with its Gift of Inquiry, drives me to share truth through this book, while Gene Key 5's Patience anchors me in the collective rhythm. As you embody your Gifts, you become a catalyst, inspiring others, as I aim to do through storytelling and coaching.

The Evolution Process: A Personal Reflection

My 7-year spiral has been a dance of unlearning and becoming. The Activation Sequence grounded me in purpose, with Gene Key 41 teaching me to dream without control. The Venus Sequence opened my heart, as Gene Key 30 healed fears of rejection, fostering authentic connections. The Pearl Sequence redefined prosperity, with Gene Key 5 guiding me to trust life's timing. Contemplating Gene Key 63's Truth, I've shifted from doubt to inquiry, trusting opportunities to arrive when I align with my design. Like opening the Gita daily, the Gene Keys is my ritual, a reminder that evolution is a spiral, drawing me closer to my true self.

Your hologenetic profile is an invitation to uncover your Gifts, soften your Shadows, and glimpse your Siddhis through contemplation. The Gene Keys is a living transmission, guiding you to a life of purpose, love, and prosperity that ripples beyond yourself. As Rudd says, "You are the pearl diver," risking everything for something greater—a truth I've found and invite you to discover.

Take Action: Start Your Gene Keys Journey

The Gene Keys is a vast, beautiful system, but you don't need to explore it all at once. Begin with a single, gentle step, letting curiosity light the way, just as I do with my daily Gita ritual. Here are three simple ways to start, each an invitation to uncover your inner wisdom:

Explore the Activation Sequence: Get your Hologenetic Profile (at genekeys.com or through a Gene Keys guide) and dive into the Activation Sequence, which covers your four Prime Gift Gene Keys—Life's Work, Evolution, Radiance, and Purpose. If the full sequence feels daunting, start with your Life's Work Gene Key—the one tied to your Personality Sun in your profile. Find its description in Richard Rudd's Gene Keys book or online (genekeys.com), exploring its Shadow, Gift, and Siddhi. For a few days, notice where these energies appear—maybe in your goals or daily choices. I began with Gene Key 41, seeing how Anticipation shaped my coaching. Write a sentence about what comes up, like a spark of insight.

Try a Gita-Like Contemplation Practice: Grab a copy of Gene Keys by Richard Rudd, open it to any page, and read the Gene Key you land on, trusting it's meant for you today. Spend five minutes reflecting—read its Shadow, Gift, and Siddhi, or journal a question like, "What does this Gene Key reveal about me now?" For me, landing on Gene Key 63's Truth felt like a call to ask, "What's true for me today?" Notice what feelings or ideas arise, as if the universe is whispering back.

These steps are your first brushstrokes on the canvas of the Gene Keys. Like opening the Gita each morning, let contemplation be a gentle ritual that awakens your light. What emerges is yours to discover—a quiet step on your unique spiral.

CHAPTER 10

NLP AND THREE A's – REWRITING YOUR PROGRAM

Life doesn't just happen—it carves us, sometimes with a gentle hand, sometimes with a blade. By the time I reached the poetic revelations of the Gene Keys, my energy had softened. It was a change I could sense—like a quiet song playing beneath the surface of my awareness. The cracks life had made in me weren't new; I'd spent years mapping them, trying to decode them. Tools like Human Design, astrology, the Enneagram, and the Gene Keys became my companions, each offering a mirror to reflect the fragments of myself I'd lost along the way. My losses weren't small but each stripped away a layer of who I thought I was, leaving me with a question that echoed louder than any answer: Who am I without all this? Rebuilding from that void isn't about reclaiming what was—it's about writing a new story, one that honors the life I choose to live.

Victor Frankl, who survived the unimaginable horrors of Nazi concentration camps, wrote, "Between stimulus and response there is a space. In that space is our power to choose our response. In our response lies our growth and our freedom." This idea has become my lifeline. We can't control what breaks us—loss, betrayal, upheaval—but we can choose the narrative we build from it. Words aren't passive; they're the architects of our reality, shaping how we see ourselves and the world. Neuro-Linguistic Programming (NLP) enters here, not as a departure from the spiritual tools I'd embraced, but as a bridge to make them actionable. If our identity rests on stories, and stories rest on words, NLP gives us the tools to take the pen and rewrite—transforming pain into purpose, loss into liberation.

From Skepticism to Curiosity: An Internal Odyssey

I wasn't always open to this path of self-exploration. My Aquarius Sun thrives on logic and innovation—tangible threads I can pull apart and reweave. Spirituality felt like a leap too far, a realm for dreamers, not doers. Astrology? Star charts seemed more decorative than directive. Human Design? A system claiming I'm a Generator who should wait rather than chase my ambitions and desires felt counterintuitive to my relentless drive. The Enneagram's personality-typing struck me as a box I didn't want to fit into, and the Gene Keys' poetic musings felt like riddles without answers. But life has a way of nudging us beyond our comfortable edges. When Arjun passed, when my marriage dissolved, when my career crumbled, the left-brain solutions I clung to—plans, strategies, fixes—fell short. Grief and loss don't bend to logic alone. That's when curiosity crept in, a quiet invitation to explore what I'd dismissed.

Each tool became a stepping stone. Human Design taught me my Generator energy thrives when I respond to life's invitations, not when I force the wheel to turn. Astrology revealed why my Aquarius Sun pushes boundaries, craving radical change to disrupt what's stale, while my Sagittarius Moon seeks the bigger picture, chasing expansive truths and philosophical meaning. These impulses clashed when my Aquarius drive to break rules felt reckless to my Sagittarius yearning for a cohesive vision, or when my Moon's restless quest for wisdom wandered too far from my Sun's focus on tangible reform. Until I understood their dance through astrology, I felt torn between rebellion and exploration.

The Enneagram was a revelation: I'd lived as an 8, a Challenger, masking my true 2w3 nature—a Helper with Achiever tendencies, giving to be loved, achieving to be seen. The Gene Keys turned my Gate 41—restless dreaming—into a gift, not a flaw. These weren't just theories; they were mirrors, reflecting my design, my conditioning, my story. Through them, I've developed my own insights—ways to use these tools not as rigid doctrines, but as flexible guides to rewrite my past and shape a future that fits who I am now.

Beyond Arjun: The Cumulative Losses

Arjun's death was a seismic crack, but it wasn't the only one. The narrative I'd created—of a strong, capable self—unraveled across years, not just in that single loss. My marriage, once a cornerstone, dissolved into silence, leaving me untethered from a partnership I'd leaned on. My career, a tapestry of ambition and identity, collapsed under economic shifts and personal exhaustion, stripping away titles I'd worn like protective armor. Each loss peeled back a layer: wife, professional, friend. What remained was a question that laid me bare: Who am I when the roles are gone?

These weren't just events—they were erasures, dismantling the self I'd constructed. I'd defined myself by what I did, who I loved, how I felt I was seen. Without them, I felt like a ghost in my own life. But this stripping down wasn't the end—it was the beginning of seeing what lay beneath.

The Power of Stories: Shaping Reality Through Words

We're all storytellers, whether we know it or not. Every day, we weave narratives—interpreting a silence, a setback, a spark—into a plot that makes sense of the chaos. These stories aren't passive; they sculpt our reality. After my losses piled up, I told myself that I'd lost everything that had defined me, and the world echoed back—emptiness where connection once stood, silence where purpose once thrummed. Yet when I shifted to a process of uncovering who I am beneath it all, stories of possibility emerged. Words carry that power. They don't just describe our experience; they create it. This chapter explores how to rewrite those stories, using practical tools to transform pain into purpose. After focusing on the Gene Keys' ethereal wisdom, I craved action—tasks my logical mind could grasp to ground my newfound faith. Neuro-Linguistic Programming (NLP) and the Three A's—Awareness, Acceptance, Action—answered that call. NLP, a self-directed practice, empowers us to rewire thoughts and emotions. The Three A's track progress, ensuring our story aligns with our true self, the authentic flow of our core energy. While tools like Enneagram, Astrology, Human Design, and Gene Keys unveil this energy, NLP and the Three A's guide us to check our progress and consciously course-correct, paving the way for the next chapter's synthesis of all we've learned.

Rewriting the Narrative: Neuro-Linguistic Programming (NLP)

Because we are, at our core, the stories we tell ourselves, the losses I faced could have cemented a narrative of defeat, a script that kept me trapped in grief and self-doubt. But stories aren't fixed; they're malleable. We have the power to craft narratives that serve us, that lift us from patterns of pain into cycles of growth and possibility. This is where Neuro-Linguistic Programming (NLP) comes in. Far from whimsical fantasy or blind optimism, NLP offers a structured, science-based approach to rewriting our inner scripts. It's a bridge between the spiritual mirrors in tools like the Gene Keys and the practical steps we can take to transform pain into purpose.

What Is NLP?

Developed in the 1970s by Richard Bandler and John Grinder, Neuro-Linguistic Programming is a set of techniques for understanding and reprogramming the patterns that shape our thoughts, emotions, and behaviors. Neuro points to the nervous system; linguistic highlights the role of language in interpreting experiences; programming refers to rewiring habits and beliefs. Rooted in cognitive psychology, linguistics, and behavioral science, NLP explores how our internal "programming"—woven from words, images, emotions—creates our reality.

NLP was a lifeline for me. Tools like the Enneagram revealed my 2w3 (Helper) nature, and the Gene Keys transformed my Gate 41's restlessness into a gift. But insight needed action. NLP aligns with this book's truth: we are energy, emotions are the language of energy, and energy lives in the body. NLP works with this triad—language shifts emotions, visualizations redirect energy, physical triggers anchor patterns somatically. It's self-directed, empowering me to rewrite my story.

At first, my skeptical side questioned NLP's claims. Critics call it pseudoscience, but its principles draw on neuroplasticity, cognitive behavioral therapy, and somatic markers (emotions tied to bodily sensations). NLP's tools transformed my life, blending the practical and profound. It's the bridge I needed after the Gene Keys, grounding faith with tasks my mind could grasp.

Three Minds: The Conscious, Unconscious, and Higher Conscious

NLP maps the mind into three realms, and understanding them unlocked new layers of my journey:

Conscious Mind: The thinking, reasoning part—only 10% of our mental landscape. It's the "why" machine, analyzing, questioning, trying to make sense of it all.

Unconscious Mind: The vast 90%, running on autopilot. It stores memories, habits, emotions, and instincts. It's where chemical reactions—like the peptides storing emotions in our bodies—shape how we feel and react.

Higher Conscious Mind: The intuitive, spiritual layer—connected to what Carl Jung called the collective unconscious. It's the gut feeling, the whisper of something bigger.

How Stories Form: The Filters of Perception

The unconscious mind is our genie, granting wishes without judgment. It takes everything literally. Tell it "I'm not enough," and it delivers self-doubt. But, tell it "I am enough," and it rewires the script. Jung said, "Until you make the unconscious conscious, it will direct your life and you will call it fate." Our senses take in roughly 2 million bits of information per second—the sound of a child's laughter, the tightening of a chest—but our conscious mind processes only about 50 to 150 bits.[^1] The rest doesn't vanish; it's stored in the unconscious, shaping our reality beyond awareness. NLP taps into this hidden reservoir, allowing us to access and reframe the emotions and energy embedded in these experiences. To manage this overload, the unconscious filters reality through:

Distortion: Bending reality. A friend's silence becomes "They don't care," though they were busy. I distorted setbacks as failure.

Generalization: One event sets a rule. A rejection becomes "No one values me," feeding into my Helper self's approval-seeking.

Deletion: Ignoring what doesn't fit. I dismissed kind words, clinging to criticism.

These filters, stored in the unconscious, built a story of defeat—but they weren't truth. NLP showed me how to adjust the lens, revealing the energy and emotions in my body. Two experiences, described in the following sections, show how I crafted narratives to cope and rebuild, unknowingly using NLP's principles.[1]

A Lifeline in Grief

After Arjun's death, grief was a heavy feeling I couldn't express. My conscious mind, logical and restrained, couldn't process it. Subconsciously, I drew on the concept of reincarnation, a premise of my Hindu faith , telling myself he'd come back to me. I imagined his soul returning in a new form, if perhaps I had another child. This storyline wasn't a literal conviction but a lifeline, a way to keep breathing when loss felt unbearable. It carried me to the birth of my son Rajiv, a different soul, yet a continuation of love. Years later, I recognized this as a subconscious reframing—a narrative I crafted to help myself cope, shifting the energy of grief into hope. It was NLP at work, long before I knew the term, showing how the unconscious mind can weave stories that serve us.

Rediscovering Empathy

Losses hardened me, or so I thought. I identified as an Enneagram 8, the Challenger—tough, controlling, rejecting the 2's nurturer, the carer who gives from the heart. I told myself that I lacked

[1]Estimates of sensory processing (approximately 2 million bits per second) and conscious capacity (50–150 bits per second) are derived from studies in cognitive psychology, notably referenced in NLP literature by Bandler and Grinder (1975) and supported by research on attention and working memory, such as Miller's (1956) work on information processing limits. For further information, see cognitive psychologist George Miller's article: The Magical Number Seven, Plus or Minus Two: Some Limits on Our Capacity for Processing Information published in 1956 in the Psychological Review.

empathy, a narrative that felt safe, a shield against vulnerability in a world that demanded strength. This story, built on deletion—ignoring moments of care—and distortion—amplifying my hardness—served me until it didn't. In an NLP-inspired workshop, a shadow-integration process, rooted in Jungian psychology, changed everything.

Shadow integration involves exploring the unconscious to embrace repressed aspects of the self. In a relaxed state, during the Enneagram workshop, I let emotions surface, and a memory emerged: as a teenager, I organized a charity drive for an old age home. I rallied friends, collected funds, and felt quiet joy—not for praise, but for giving. This memory, buried in my unconscious, proved my heart was alive. I hadn't lacked empathy; caring was at my core, suppressed as a coping mechanism to build a "tough" identity. Reframing this, I accepted my 2w3 (Helper) truth: "I'm not cold; I'm empathetic, choosing when to give." The weight in my chest lifted, my energy softened. This was NLP's power—making the unconscious conscious, aligning my story with my body's truth.

NLP Tools: Self-Directed Practices to Rewrite Your Story

NLP's power lies in self-directed tools you learn and practice, shifting thoughts, language, and the body to transform emotional energy. After embracing my true narrative—the story of living aligned with my authentic energetic self, forged through shadow integration and self-discovery—these are some of the NLP tools I used to build my new narrative and reshape my story consciously:

1. Reframing: Changing the Lens

What It Is: Reframing means looking at a situation or belief in a new way. It's like putting a different frame around a picture—the image stays the same, but how you see it changes.

How to Use It: Ask yourself, "What else could this mean?" or "How can I view this differently?" This shifts your perspective and softens emotional triggers.

Why It Helps: It turns negative or limiting thoughts into neutral or positive ones, freeing you from mental ruts.

I reframed my story from "I'm stuck" (feeling trapped) and "I must help others to be loved" (a 2w3 Helper pattern) to "I'm aligning with the right opportunity" and "I help when I'm whole." These shifts honor my need to give while protecting my energy.

2. Anchoring: Tying a Feeling to a Trigger

What It Is: Anchoring connects a specific feeling (like calmness or hopefulness) to a physical action (like squeezing your thumb). It lets you call up that feeling whenever you need it.

How to Use It: Recall a time you felt the desired emotion, fully feel it, then pair it with a trigger (e.g., a touch). Repeat until the trigger brings back the feeling.

Why It Helps: It's a quick way to shift your emotional state, giving you control in tough moments.

I set up a physical trigger. I squeeze my thumb to feel hope instead of restlessness—a reminder as a 2w3 that I'm enough without overgiving. So when emotions run high, this anchor pulls me back to a steady, hopeful state.

3. Swish Pattern: Replacing Old Images

What It Is: The swish pattern is a visualization trick to swap a negative mental image for a positive one.

How to Use It: Picture the old, unwanted image (e.g., you, feeling stressed). Then imagine a new, empowering image (e.g., you, in a calm state). Mentally "swish" them—shrink the old one and grow the new image until it takes over.

Why It Helps: It rewires automatic negative thoughts, replacing them with images that empower you.

I replaced the old image of me – frantic and reactive, overwhelmed by life -- with a new image: calm, responding thoughtfully—not just reacting. I visualize this shift, blending my Aquarius vision with Sagittarius purpose.

These tools work because stories built on distortions ("I'm not enough"), generalizations ("Nothing works"), or deletions (ignoring the good) trap us. These NLP tools break through those bars: Reframing offers new perspectives, uncovering my softness beneath a thought like "Succeed or you're nothing." Now, it's "Feel, Free (respond), Flow (grow)." Anchoring rewires emotional habits, grounding me in the knowing that "I'm enough." Using the swish pattern swaps out frantic visuals for calm ones, aligning my unconscious mind with my truth.

Science and Spirit: A Bridge for Mind and Soul

NLP blends science and spirit, fitting well with my journey from skepticism to faith. My skeptical mind demanded logic. Tools like Enneagram and Human Design opened curiosity, while Gene Keys' ethereal wisdom pushed me into faith—heart over mind. NLP balanced this, giving my restless mind tasks while deepening my understanding of spiritual truths.

Science: NLP uses neuroscience—words and images trigger neural pathways. "I'm healing" fires different circuits than "I'm broken," rewiring via the brain's plasticity. Emotions, as peptides, shift with these patterns, easing bodily tension. Anchoring uses somatic markers, reframing reduces amygdala stress—tasks that my logical mind tackles.

Spirit: NLP echoes Gene Keys: every shadow hides a gift. My 2w3's (Helper's) gift is loving with boundaries. Reframing turns "I must" into "I choose"; anchoring, grounds the idea that "I'm enough"; swish pattern, aligns with calm purpose, mirroring Human Design's somatic response.

NLP transforms how I carry pain. It's self-directed, requiring only my practice. For my mind, it's a playground—rewiring thoughts, shifting energy, grounding emotions in my body. For my spirit, it's a bridge, weaving Gene Keys' faith with a Human Design Generator's response. It's empowered my 2w3 (Helper) to give from wholeness, and it can be empowering for you as well.

These tools don't erase pain—they transform how pain is carried. For me, they've balanced my Helper's heart with my Achiever's drive, turning "I must" into "I choose." They provide practical steps to rewrite your story, one thought, one feeling, one image at a time.

The Three A's Framework: A Path to Spiritual Transformation

The "Three A's of Change" is a well-established framework traditionally used in change management to guide individuals or organizations through transformation. It's not a groundbreaking concept, but its simplicity and effectiveness make it a potent tool for explaining how change happens. The framework comprises three steps: Awareness, Acceptance, and Action. In its conventional form, it's applied as follows:

Awareness: Recognizing the need for change, understanding the current situation, and identifying what must be altered. This step ensures everyone involved is informed and aligned.

Acceptance: Embracing the change by overcoming resistance, fostering commitment, and agreeing to move forward.

Action: Implementing the change through practical steps, resource allocation, and progress tracking.

For those wondering, "What do I need to do?" or "How will all this information help me?", the Three As provide a clear and actionable answer. When adapted to a spiritual context, this framework takes on a deeper, more introspective meaning, guiding us through a journey of self-discovery, healing, and alignment with our true selves. Here's how it applies:

Awareness: The Starting Point of Change

In the traditional sense, awareness is about recognizing the need for change. Spiritually, it's the foundation of transformation—it's about understanding who we are, why we are the way we are, and why we do the things we do. This self-awareness is the spark that ignites any meaningful change. To build this awareness, I've introduced tools like the Enneagram, astrology, and Human Design. These aren't abstract systems—they're practical mirrors reflecting our unique design:

Enneagram: Uncovers our core motivations and behavioral patterns.

Astrology: Reveals how cosmic influences shape our tendencies and life path.

Human Design: Maps our energetic blueprint, showing how we're wired to interact with the world.

These tools help us see beyond societal conditioning, peeling back the layers to reveal our authentic essence. For any change to happen—whether it's personal growth that shows up as mental clarity, emotional healing or spiritual awakening—awareness is the start. Without it, we're navigating in the dark. Awareness activates the prefrontal cortex and somatic attention engages the nervous system, grounding emotions as energy while aligning with NLP's filters.

Acceptance: Embracing Without Blame

Traditionally, acceptance is about committing to change and letting go of resistance. In a spiritual context, it's about acknowledging our experiences without judgment or blame. The tools that build awareness also show us how our conditioning—family, culture, past events—has shaped us. Acceptance isn't about rejecting or fixing these influences; it's about integrating them into our whole self.

This step also involves understanding the profound link between emotions, energy, and the body. Emotions aren't just thoughts—they carry frequencies that impact our energy. Low frequencies, like guilt or shame, can leave us stuck, while higher frequencies, like love or gratitude, elevate our consciousness. By accepting our emotions and experiences, we release blame—toward ourselves or others—and create space for healing. This allows us to navigate life more effectively, moving from stagnation into a flow state. Contemplating or simply reading the Gene Keys is a great way to ignite the spark of acceptance on this journey. Acceptance reduces amygdala stress, shifting the balance of peptides and allowing a move from guilt to peace, which aligns with somatic-energy and NLP's reframing of thoughts and emotions.

Action: Change That Flows Naturally

In the traditional framework, action is about taking deliberate steps to implement change. Spiritually, it's different—we're no longer merely "left-brain travelers" plotting every move. Instead, action, in a spiritual sense, unfolds as a gentle uncovering of your true self, far from the traditional model of forced, deliberate change. This is a transformation rooted in being, not doing. This is where the universe conspires to align circumstances as you embody alignment through awareness and acceptance, much like my Human Design Generator energy responds rather than initiates. We don't have to go searching for the right action—it finds us. Instead of plotting rigid plans, you trust the process, letting steps emerge—pausing to rest, anchoring a sense of "enough" with a thumb squeeze, or reframing old stories like "I'm not enough" to "I'm becoming." In this way, you are using NLP tools not to force outcomes but to catch patterns and reinforce this more harmonious state of being, consciously strengthening neural pathways through neuroplasticity to ground new narratives in your body's energy.

Cultivating higher emotions, like gratitude or love, as Donny Epstein's energetic states suggest, amplifies this flow. The high frequency of these emotions fosters heart-brain coherence to attract the right opportunities—people, events, possibilities—without effort. Your body guides you. Its signals of openness or tension revealing alignment, as when I paused my hustling, accepted my limits, and rested. I could feel my shoulders softening as inspired coaching and writing emerged not from sheer motivation or determination but from a friend's call or in the stillness of a quiet morning. I sensed the change when gratitude's warmth would rise in my chest, anchored by a heart-touch. Often, that shift would then draw a chance coffee invite and the welcome rekindling of old bonds, my energy of connection pulling others nearer. These acts—anchoring, pausing—when sprinkled throughout the day, serve as gentle reminders to stay in an aware state. This is where transformation puts you in touch with your body's truth and the universe's support. These awakened energies are weaving a path where inspired action finds you.

When we truly understand ourselves (awareness) and embrace our experiences (acceptance), energy shifts. Restless emotions settle, tense interactions are eased, people around us change, events align. It's not about forcing outcomes with rigid plans or theories—it's about trusting the process. As we align with our true selves, the universe conspires to support us, and we become the change we want to see in the world. This is the essence of the transformative process—not doing but being.

The Three A's: A Barometer for Progress

The Three A's—awareness, acceptance, action measure how aligned your story and actions are with your more expansive sense of self, guiding you to respond, not react, as Human Design's wisdom teaches. Like a compass, they can reveal when you're off course, using somatic signals (tightness or ease in your body), emotional energy (stagnation or flow), and narrative clarity (limiting or empowering stories) to prompt adjustments. If awareness uncovers a story like "I'm not enough" but acceptance feels blocked—perhaps a tight chest or lingering guilt—you can course-correct with NLP tools, such as reframing, to create a shift toward expansiveness and the release of old programming.

If moving toward action feels forced, like pushing through tension, you then can revisit awareness to check somatic cues, allowing you to ensure that your steps align with your Generator (Human Design) energy's responsive flow rather than moving into a reactive stance. This feedback loop, grounded in the body-emotion-energy triad, transforms pain into purpose by keeping your narrative and actions true. For example, when my business collapsed, awareness revealed my 2w3 (Enneagram) story: "I'm failing, unworthy without success," with my chest tight and panic surging. Acceptance began with reframing—"This is a pivot, not a loss"—easing my breath slightly, but a sense of guilt lingered, a sign I hadn't fully embraced the shift. In terms of action, I used NLP's swish pattern, visualizing a vivid image of frantic failure—me scrambling, overwhelmed—and rapidly shrinking it to a tiny, dim speck while expanding a bright, compelling image of calm confidence—me steady, purposeful—in its place, repeating this five times daily for a week. My body relaxed noticeably, and I paused my hustle, journaling: "I choose to respond."

Coaching emerged naturally from my connected state, yet, when I later pushed coaching too hard, tension returned, my shoulders rigid, guilt resurfacing. The A's signaled I'd skipped the process of full acceptance as I was rushing to prove my worth. I revisited acceptance, reframing more deeply: "Loss frees me to create anew." Feeling my chest soften, I rested, anchored in the concept of "enough," and flow returned—coaching grew authentically, clients drawn to my presence. This cycle, looping through body and emotion, ensures that you craft a story that serves, responding to life's cues with grace.

I use the Three A's to gauge progress. I consider it a cycle, not a checklist, flowing from insight to a life that feels true to my core. The Three As integrate NLP, Human Design, Enneagram, and Gene Keys, weaving mind, body, spirit. Awareness reveals what was hidden, acceptance shifts emotional energy, action grounds somatically. They break through cages of our own creation—distortions, generalizations, deletions—echoing NLP's filters.

My old script, "Succeed or you're nothing," buried my softness. The new, "Feel, Free, Flow," holds all that is true, reflected in my body's responses. As we apply and integrate the Three As, life becomes a dance of self-discovery.

For me, the healing state wasn't found through trying out one tool—it was through reaching into a tool chest. The Enneagram reframed my identity by revealing my 2w3's unconscious drive to seek worth through helping, allowing me to embrace my authentic self beyond approval-seeking roles. Human Design showed me how to respond authentically as a Generator, aligning my energy with intuitive flow rather than forced action. The Gene Keys allowed me to transform my shadows like fear of unworthiness, into gifts of self-acceptance, revealing my inherent potential. NLP made it practical by providing tools to rewrite limiting stories into empowering narratives of choice and clarity. Together, they uncovered the real me—not the old roles, but the person beneath. This chapter equips you with NLP and the Three A's—tools to rewrite and track your story. The next chapter weaves all learnings into a unified path, shaping a life that's yours to choose.

Take Action: Track Your Story

Try the Three A's:

Awareness: Pick an unwanted story that circulates in your head—e.g, "I can't slow down." Notice your body—tension, breath. Write: "I tell myself ___."

Acceptance: Feel somatically—where and how do you feel it, chest, gut. Reframe or contemplate.

Action: Choose an action step to improve this story—pause 10 minutes, anchor in a state of calm. Write: "I choose ___." Check in with your body—aligned? Adjust. Repeat weekly. I reframed "I'm broken" to "I'm becoming," felt my body soften, pivoted to coaching.

Share your new story—speaking it makes it real.

CHAPTER 11

CRAFTING THE NARRATIVE – FROM RESISTANCE TO PURPOSE

This is my perfect moment, sitting on the balcony of my Singapore home, a steaming coffee mug in my hands. The mug, a treasured gift from a dear old friend, glows with intricate gold and yellow designs, its elegance a quiet reminder of our warm connection. As I take my first sip, the rich taste and perfect warmth are waking my senses. The gentle morning breeze brushes my skin, carrying the delicate scent of the magnolias blooming below. I bask in this stillness, as gratitude washes over me for this journey, uniquely mine. It was here, within this ephemeral scene, that I truly grasped the meaning of happiness.

I once struggled with the New Age call for a daily gratitude ritual, especially on days—or weeks—when loss and pain clouded my heart. After life's repeated upheavals, I'd found stability—no new worries, strong family ties despite a dissolved marriage, a comfortable life even after the family business's downgrade—but

I felt I'd earned this respite, so listing these constants daily for gratitude seemed pointless and naive, their sameness offering nothing new to stir my heart. But then I heard it stated so eloquently: happiness is nothing but little moments of joy—not grand victories, but small, shimmering details waiting to be noticed.

I'd had coffee on this balcony before, but it hadn't meant so much until that morning, when I paused and truly saw what was before me. I noticed how beautiful the magnolias were, their soft petals catching light, their fragrance a subtle gift; the mug's delicate patterns under my fingers; the coffee's warmth and taste stirring me awake. Each detail bloomed into joy, and the more I noticed, the more I appreciated. The more I appreciated each detail, the more I found to be grateful for.

With my increasing awareness, I started noticing everything in my path—a stranger's smile, a quiet evening's glow. Ease and presence crept into my consciousness, day by day, weaving a tapestry of well-being. These moments showed me how energy flows when we pause to feel it and lifted me from apathy to the higher vibration of joy. This happiness, born not from external triumphs but from within, had emerged on the winding path of my journey, a light kindled by seeing the small and savoring the moment.

I'm calmer, at peace now. My experiences described in Chapter 11 left me with a sense of stillness—no longer restless, I was now watching my energy become something freer than it's ever been. I'd peeled back layers as I released my skepticism and began letting tools like the Enneagram, astrology and Human

Design help me to rewrite my story. These tools showed me I am energy, and my purpose is to express it freely. The achiever's protective armor was gone, the survivor's edge softened, and I'd landed in this moment: not forcing the wheel to turn, just cruising along. But this ride wasn't always calm. I once fought hard against the path I now am on—coaching. I despised it at first. It felt too passive, not enough action involved to keep me engaged. Me, as an advisor? It felt like a big step down from the days when I challenged the CEOs who sat across from me at board tables. Yet here I am, guiding people to their truest and highest potential, crafting narratives that liberate, not limit. This chapter traces that transformative journey—elucidating how I went from resistance to purpose, and how every tool pulled me closer to where I stand now.

The Wall of Resistance

Rewind a decade. Coaching wasn't even a blip on my horizon. Even after my exit from the family business when friends suggested coaching – I swatted it away, like a fly. I'd built my life in the family business, a world of ledgers and wins, my assertive hum cutting through the noise like a blade. Business leader, dealmaker—those were my badges, forged through logic, not feelings. I remember the weight of a fountain pen in my hand, signing a contract that saved a sinking division, the air in the boardroom thick with tension and triumph. That was me—a doer, not a dreamer. This resistance was my conditioning blocking the flow of my true energy. When life hit hard—Arjun's death, the empire unraveling—I didn't soften; I armored up, the survivor in me rising up. Coaching? That was for people who sat still, not me. I didn't want to advise; I wanted to build.

Practicality fueled my years of resistance, too. My scorecard for success was money. People preached to me about the importance of having an impact—"change lives!"—but my life was the family business, my legacy. Coaching wouldn't match the revenue of a deal well struck, I told myself. And empathy? I thought I lacked it. Who was I to "help" anyone? I'd spent decades proving myself through results—profit margins, not pep talks. Yet something gnawed at me. Arjun's absence wasn't just a loss; it was a signal. The business collapse wasn't failure; it was a shove. And the tools I'd stumbled into and the lessons I had learned kept whispering back, louder each time, until I couldn't ignore them.

What I Do Now

These days, I guide others to uncover their life's purpose, helping them consciously weave their unique essence into every corner of their existence—work, relationships, and the quiet moments in between. Life isn't a set of silos, but a vibrant, intermingled flow, and my coaching nurtures connections across it all, so clients can show up authentically. I share my journey—from skeptic and entrepreneur to coach—blending tools like Enneagram, astrology, and Human Design to spark self-discovery in my clients and to hold space for their own wisdom to emerge. Their purpose, like mine, is to express their unique energy authentically. What matters isn't just what they do, but how their quality of being shines through. My privilege is witnessing hearts open and lives align, as my clients step into a purpose that feels like home.

We Are Energy: From Skepticism to Acceptance

After weaving through the intricate threads of Enneagram, astrology, Human Design , Gene Keys, NLP, and more, the essential message of my journey emerges clear and bold. Here's the heartbeat of it all: We are energy—cosmic and vibrant—uniquely imprinted in each of us.

My greatest breakthrough came when I acknowledged that truth: we are energy, a living current woven with a purpose—the call to express our unique energetic essence. As a skeptic, my heart once clenched against anything that didn't bend to logic. Physics taught me the laws of energy in school, but the notion that we are energy—vibrating, cosmic, pulsing with the intent to live authentically—felt like a leap I couldn't make. I'd been exposed to ideas about the soul, sensed we were more than what our daily grind represented, but who pauses to feel it from one moment to the next? Like hamsters on a wheel, we function on autopilot, only noticing the hum of our essence in rare silences or when life cracks us open.

For me, that crack was a thunderstorm—grief and loss shaking my world awake. But it needn't be so fierce. New age guru, Deepak Chopra offers a gentler take: ask, "Who am I? Why am I here? What is my purpose?" These questions, held softly as a breath in the chest, unravel the roles we wear and call forth answers. When I whispered, "Who am I, stripped of titles?," life answered—not with words, but with a pulsing current I felt in my veins during workshops, the energy, warm and real, urging me to explore further.

This journey doesn't require tragedy. If you feel that dreaded wheel starting to spin, pause. Turn within and ask Chopra's questions—"Who am I? Why am I here? What is my purpose?" to yourself. They are a lifeline to step off before life finds ways to jolt you awake. Our purpose as humans is to engage with every facet of our energy, to remove blockages and let our unique current ripple through us like a story unfolding, rich and unhurried. By asking these questions, we invite the dance, our heart's rhythm guiding us to live not merely as matter, but as light.

Cosmic Cocktails: Unique Blends of the Cosmos

That light within each of us sparks a question: if we're all energy, are we the same or does each soul carry a distinctive pattern? My yoga retreats had stirred awareness of a warm current within me, revealing we're not just bodies but a living essence that transcends flesh. The Enneagram, my first step, offered a map—simple, almost too practical, like a left-brain's guide to the heart's mystery. It sorts our energy into types, each driven by a unique quality—love, truth, courage. This method seems to be cloaking mysticism in a psychological framework, unproven yet alive with insight.

Enneagram gave me a basic framework showing I'm a Helper with an Achiever's edge—not just a doer, but a feeler too. This was my unique energy stated in basic terms. Astrology deepened my understanding that we're each unique expressions, our essence shaped by the location of the stars and planets at birth. We vibrate as one in Source yet resonate with a distinct song. Astrology showed my unique blend.

Each of us is a singular cocktail, a vibrant blend of the cosmic energy as the base spirit, with emotions swirling like spices that dance across the palate. This unique concoction is crafted with an innate capacity to savor every note of life's melody. Our energy, the essence that fuels us, mixes with the flavors of our experiences—joy as bright as citrus, sorrow as deep as aged whiskey, and hope as effervescent as a splash of tonic. Just as a master mixologist balances ingredients to create a drink that lingers on the tongue, we unfold as an energy puzzle, each moment a chance to refine our recipe. With awareness and heartfelt intention, we can elevate our harmonious range, aligning with our essential selves to craft a life that resonates like a perfectly poured cocktail, each sip revealing a new layer of our unique dance.

Emotions: The Notes of Your Song

If we are all energy, as Richard Rudd suggests, our genius is "that radiant essence born to spill into the world."[^2] This essence finds its voice through our emotions, the vibrant notes that compose the symphony of our being. Each emotion—every tear, laugh, or quiet ache—plays a distinct role, like strings, brass, or percussion in an orchestra. Joy may soar like a violin's crescendo, while grief grounds us like the deep hum of a cello. These notes, when allowed to flow freely, tune the pitch of our purpose, guiding us toward alignment with our truest selves.[2]

The beauty of this inner symphony lies in its diversity. No single note defines the music; rather, it's the interplay

[2]Rudd, Richard. Gene Keys: Unlocking the Higher Purpose Hidden in Your DNA. Watkins Publishing, 2013.

of emotions—clashing, blending, resolving—that creates a masterpiece. Imagine a symphony where only one instrument plays: it would lack depth, movement, and soul. Similarly, suppressing or favoring one emotion over others mutes our range. By embracing every note, from the sharp sting of anger to the soft whisper of contentment, we allow our spirit to dance through us. The conductor—our conscious awareness—orchestrates these notes, ensuring they harmonize rather than compete. When we listen to our emotions without judgment, they become a compass, each vibration signaling the needs of our energy, guiding us toward a life that resonates with purpose and authenticity. But why emotions? Why not will or logic? Because emotions are energy's language, and expressing them, from the heaviest to the lightest, refines our melody, aligning us with the truth of who we are.

David Hawkins taught me this first, mapping emotions like a ladder of light. Lower emotions—shame, heavy as a stone in the gut, or fear, a tight knot in the chest—vibrate low, draining our life force, locking us in shadows. Hawkins' scale, from 1 to 1,000, shows shame at 20, fear at 100, but love at 500, joy at 540, soaring high, amplifying our energy. You can't leap to joy without wading through fear's mud, feeling it, naming it, letting it pass. My own grief, a weight I carried after loss, held me in low vibrations until I let it spill, tears loosening the knot, lifting me toward peace. Suppressing lower emotions traps us; expressing them—raw, unjudged—frees the current, unblocking a stream, letting higher notes of love and courage flow.

Clare Graves' spiral of consciousness expands this truth, showing why higher emotions matter. His model, a winding path of human evolution, maps how we climb through emotional layers—survival's fear, power's anger, community's empathy, integration's clarity. Each rung, from raw instinct to holistic purpose, resonates with a higher emotional pitch. Lower emotions, like anger's fire, keep us stuck in ego's grip; higher ones, like compassion's warmth, align us with our true self. You can't find your purpose in fear's low drone—you need love's clear chime. Graves' spiral isn't linear; we climb, we slip, but never fall all the way down, each step etching wisdom into our auric field. My own journey mirrored this, anger giving way to acceptance, each emotional note a step toward coaching's call.

Donny Epstein's "The Seeker's Code" brought this home, framing emotions as energies we refine, like perfecting a musical pitch. His stages—Bio Energy, raw and survival-driven, pulsing with fear or stress; Transform Energy, emotional currents of grief or courage; Soul Energy, love and purpose's high vibrations—form a spiral, much like Graves'. To evolve, we express Bio's heavy notes, letting Transform's shifts carry us to Soul's radiant song. Epstein says this is internal, within our auric field. My experiences showed me this: feeling anger's heat, then love's warmth, tuned my energy to guide others.

Richard Rudd's Gene Key 22, with its map of bodies, echoes this wisdom. Beyond our physical frame, we hold an astral body, where emotions swirl, and a causal body, where love and grace resonate, tying us to purpose. Higher bodies, subtler still, hum with unity's song. These aren't distant states—they're within our aura, layered energies we tap by feeling our way through. Hindu traditions describe this: prana, life's energy, flows through centers like the heart's Anahata, where love lifts us, or the root's Muladhara, where fear grounds us. Lower emotions, tied to tamas' inertia, block prana; higher ones, sattva's harmony, let it soar. My yoga practice, breath syncing with my heart's pulse, taught me to feel fear, then love, prana flowing freer like the sound of a beautiful note expressed.

Here's the secret: this spiral—Hawkins' ladder, Graves' path, Epstein's energies, Rudd's bodies, Hinduism's prana—lives within us. We don't need external sparks; our aura holds every note, from shame's low hum to joy's clear bell. Expressing emotions, high and low, is how we climb, refining our pitch to play the music that's truly ours. Like a melody with just the right tones, each feeling adds depth, each release a step toward our inherent genius.

Body and Conditioning: The Vessel of Our Song

If clarifying our emotions brings us into harmony with our energy's purpose, how does our body, the vessel, shape this song, and what constricts its flow? Human Design and Gene Keys reveal our bodies as uniquely crafted to house our distinct energy, yet life's conditioning tends to disrupt a smooth current. Human Design speaks of neutrinos—elusive cosmic particles streaming from stars, imprinting us at birth with an energetic signature, like a fingerprint of the cosmos. Science hasn't stamped it "proven" yet, but it's tangible enough to grip onto symbolically. These neutrinos encode both our "hardware"—the body's form—and our "software"—the soul's essence—molding us as singular expressions of universal energy.

Human Design maps this through channels and gates, pathways in a BodyGraph that guide energy's flow, unique to each of us. My Generator design, with gates like 41 sparking imagination, channels energy through response, not force. Masaru Emoto showed water—our body's essence—shifts with emotions, love forming radiant crystals, fear revealing chaos. Candace Pert and Bruce Lipton deepened this understanding: emotions trigger neuropeptides, binding to cells, while stress or love alters DNA expression, tying heart to health. Unexpressed emotions kink the flow, dimming our vessel's light. My resistance to coaching, fists clenched after Arjun's loss and the business collapse, stuffed anger down, my body tense, misaligned.

Gene Keys sees this process through the lens of DNA as a poetic transducer of cosmic light. Neutrinos activate our gates—64 codons, mirroring Human Design. This activation affects our biochemistry, our DNA responding with a spark of vitality. Shadows—low-frequency patterns that emerge with feelings of doubt or a need to assert control—kink this flow, etched during childhood or through interactions with others. We're bombarded by cosmic and human energies—family expectations, cultural norms—twisting our hose, through conditioning or not self-patterns, as Human Design calls it. When our conditioning takes over our energy stalls.

Our bodies can be seen as perfect hoses, designed to let our unique and authentic energy flow unhindered and free. Richard Rudd says we're born geniuses and that our purpose is to share this radiance through our singular vessel. Picture water rushing through a hose, smooth and clear—that's our energy, designed to move naturally, emotions its voice, coded by DNA's dance. But life kinks the hose. Conditioning—Human Design's "not-self" patterns, Gene Keys' shadow frequencies—obstructs the flow. Conditioning is the patterns that block our energy, like kinks in a hose.

Our emotions reveal these kinks, our energy's need for release. Stuff the emotions, and the hose tightens; lash out, and it tangles. Observing them lets us see what's ours and what's not—separating out others' energies, societal scripts. Human Design's methodical Strategy and Authority—my Generator's gut response—guides this flow, precise as a compass. Gene Keys, with poetic wisdom, invites contemplation to shift shadows to gifts, unlocking DNA's hidden code. Awareness of these conditioned tendencies allows our genius to sing clearly through a vessel designed for us. This journey, kinked yet sacred, leads us to rewrite our stories, a dance of deconditioning.

Deconditioning: Unkinking the Hose

If our body is the hose and our unique energy the water, how do we unkink it? We let our genius flow not by chasing perfection, but by expressing emotions authentically and with ease, moment by moment. This is conscious deconditioning—releasing the vestiges of old patterns by choice. I learned this after my losses, my heart clenched, resisting any subtle urges toward the practice of coaching. Those obstructions weren't of my own creation alone. Life weaves them, through childhood rules, the energetic influence of others and also societal conditioning. In Hinduism, all of this forms the Maya, the illusion that blinds us, wrapping our true energy in stories of shame or striving, as if we're not already whole.

Donny Epstein's Network Spinal Analysis offers a temporary fix, using gentle spinal touches to release conditioning's grip, like a rush of water clearing years of silt. I felt it in workshops, my body softening, energy pulsing more freely. Yet Network Spinal Analysis, for all its power, is a practitioner's tool—a left-brain step, handing agency to another. It's a key to unlock, not a path to walk. True deconditioning, the kind that keeps the hose clear, comes from within, through crafting our own story. This is where our power lies, not in tools or guides, but in our free will to choose the narrative that expresses our truth.

The past holds the residue—every loss, every role I clung to, like the "doer" who scoffed at stillness. Accepting it all, without judgment, was my first step toward releasing the flow. Every experience, from grief's weight to triumphs' shine, led me here, to this moment, to express my radiant purpose. No blame, no regret—just a nod to life's design, each challenge shaping my genius, as Richard Rudd calls it. NLP became my pen, reframing old tales—loss as lessons, limits as doors—while Human Design's passenger mindset taught me to observe, not drive. I watch my emotions, my kinks, like scenery passing by, not mine to control but merely to feel. Gene Keys' poetic wisdom, meanwhile, nudged me awake enough to see shadows—fear, control—as Maya's veil, not my essence.

Tools like Enneagram, astrology, Human Design, Gene Keys, NLP—they're mirrors, not masters. They help us see our unique energy, the unique spirit that we are. Trouble brews when we cling too tightly, however, letting tools or stories become a new form of conditioning. With complete acceptance, we dismantle Maya's old narratives—blame, victimhood—and build anew, each emotion becoming a note in a melody that serves our purpose. This isn't a one-time fix; it's maintenance, a daily choice to observe, feel, and reframe, keeping the hose clear.

Our purpose, then, is to let our energy flow, authentic and unhindered, through a body made for us. Every challenge, every shadow, provides a chance to consciously engage, to choose. This is free will in action, with its capacity to pierce Maya's illusion. By accepting our past and crafting stories that align with our genius, we step into faith, trusting the next harmonious note of our song will emerge. This dance of deconditioning is how purpose aligns with our truest energy, a melody with just the right notes.

From Resistance to Purpose: My Journey

Rewind to me seated peacefully on the balcony, coffee warm in my hands, the fragrance of magnolias wafting up from the tree below. I was unhappy with coaching—it felt too passive and like a demotion from the head of the boardroom. I'd been a business leader, a survivor, not an advisor. Yet here I am now, guiding my clients to reach their full potential, sharing my story and my insights. Complete self-acceptance was the key, swallowing my pride was the leap. Coaching wasn't a lesser role—it was mine to embrace. My 2w3 balanced Helper with Achiever. My

Scriptwriter vocation crafted their stories. My stars aligned—Aquarius innovation, Sagittarius depth. This is my spiritual path: engaging with maps that work, not acting on blind faith.

The Essentials, Restated

So, the essential message? We're unique energy mixes, imprinted by the cosmos—neutrinos, stars, DNA—housed in vessels designed to express it. Life's purpose is alignment, and letting that energy flow freely. Unblocked emotions flow through the hose, lifting us to higher consciousness for the soul's greatest ride. Tools like HD, Gene Keys, and NLP help us to rewrite the story, guiding us back to ourselves.

Take Action

No steps here—just be. Sit with your energy, let it hum. Notice your breath, the quiet, the noise—whatever's there. Don't steer it; observe it, a passenger taking in the view. That's it: being, right now.

CHAPTER 12

BEYOND THE VEIL – SYNCHRONICITY, ENERGY, AND THE GAME OF LIFE

So much has changed for me. Now, I carry the calmness with me. No more restless pacing—just a sense of inner quiet that feels like a reward after a long climb. This book has been a map of how I arrived at this place. It began with the Raja Yoga that jolted me awake. Then, the Enneagram started the process of peeling back my layers. David Hawkins fine-tuned my energy, Human Design sketched the blueprint of my soul, Gene Keys wove poetic insights, and Neurolinquistic Programming handed me tools to rewrite my inner script. I began as Nisha—the skeptic, the doer, the Indian girl who built a business on logic and scoffed at anything too "woo-woo." Life threw its punches—my world collapsing—and I morphed into the survivor, chin up, unbroken. Now? I'm not just those fragments. I'm all of me, freer than I ever imagined possible. But let me be clear: this chapter isn't for the skeptics. If "woo-woo" triggers you, as it once did me not so long ago, I suggest you pause here. But if you're an intrepid spiritual seeker, as I've become, read on.

Encouraged by the changes I was noticing within as I progressed in my journey, I began stepping away from skepticism. I started to wonder: what else had I been rejecting? My transformation wasn't something I forced into being. I could puff up my chest and claim I chose this path, but that's not the truth. It unfolded organically. People, moments, and clarity fell into place without me wrestling them into submission. That's the essence of this book: how, by clearing my emotions and ascending to higher ones, I found the right type of energy to face whatever came next. If I hadn't, I'd still be trapped, replaying the same tired dramas with fresh faces and new backdrops. Instead, I shifted, and the world shifted with me. Synchronicity became my compass, and life began to feel less like a brutal fight and more like a game—one I could level up in, step by step.

The Journey: Stumbling into Synchronicity

Let's rewind to where the shift in my perspective began. I didn't orchestrate any of this—no grand plan of mine guided me to the workshops or tools that changed me. Take the yoga workshop: I went because I wasn't working and needed an escape from the chaos of the family business. Years earlier, a friend had nudged me toward the same event—I'd even paid—but I bailed at the last second, wary of the guru and his rituals. This time, with no meetings or excuses to hide behind, I showed up. The wellness retreat? Another friend dragged me along, promising weight loss and rest after work stress had run me ragged. I wasn't expecting chakra balancing or anything remotely spiritual. Hoffman? It surfaced in a casual chat with a friend who raved about it. I didn't even know what it was, and the online reviews were so strange that I nearly backed out. The Enneagram workshop? A friend couldn't attend and passed me her spot.

Do you see the pattern? I didn't chase these experiences—they landed in my lap. And sometimes, in spite of myself, things started to click. It wasn't instant enlightenment. No workshop handed me my sense of purpose on a silver platter. But gradually, like puzzle pieces snapping together, the right people and circumstances appeared. At a retreat, someone recommended a book that shifted my perspective. A workshop conversation sparked an idea that lingered. My old way of being in the world unraveled slowly, and I had the spaciousness within to notice—my mind wasn't cluttered anymore. I could think, feel, see and be fully present. The more I paid attention to the seeming coincidences, the more these synchronicities stacked up. It was like finding the loose end of a tangled string of yarn—suddenly, life felt less frustrating and more navigable.

One moment stands out vividly. I was at a business event in Singapore. Seated with four strangers, we skipped the small talk and dove straight into life, purpose, the raw, messy stuff. One of them mentioned being fascinated by "The Celestine Prophecy," by James Redfield. I nodded politely. I had read the book years ago and it hadn't left much of an impression on me. Months later, I read the book once again. This time around I noticed it to be about the power of synchronicity. This was a description of what I'd been living without even realizing. The connection hit me like a thunderbolt, revealing how these unscripted moments had been gently steering me all along.

Synchronicity: When the Universe Lines Up

The Oxford Dictionary defines synchronicity as "the simultaneous occurrence of events which appear significantly related but have no discernible causal connection." [^3] It's more than luck, though—it's alignment. It's the universe winking at you when you're tuned in. Human Design talks about the magnetic monopole, that invisible force within that draws synchronicity into our lives. Life is designed to be synchronous—it's we who throw it off course. How? By failing to align our energy and our bodies with our natural state. Life, at its core, is about returning to that essence, remembering who we truly are. And it's no easy feat. We're constantly bombarded by energies that aren't ours—cosmic transits (think astrology's predictions) and the energy fields of others. During any particular astrological transit, you might hear how certain planetary movements impact different star signs in unique ways. And when it comes to others' energy, sometimes it's subtle, but often it's a trigger. But here's the reminder, once again: it's not about them—it's about you.[3]

David Hawkins would frame it in terms of energy levels. He mapped out emotions on a scale: shame at 20, fear at 100, courage at 200, love at 500, peace at 700. The lower ones drag you down, heavy and sluggish; the higher ones lift you, light and expansive. When I was mired in grief (75) after Arjun's death or clinging to

[3]Oxford English Dictionary. Oxford University Press, 2023.

pride (175) with the business, life reflected that—chaos, walls, dead ends. As I cleared those weights, climbing to acceptance (350) or reason (400), the world transformed. People appeared. Doors opened. I didn't have to force them—they swung wide on their own.

It's not "woo-woo"—it's physics, in a way. Hawkins argued emotions are frequencies, measurable energy. Shame vibrates low, a sluggish hum; love vibrates high, a clear, resonant note. Shift your energy, and what you attract shifts, too. I didn't muscle my way into these synchronicities—they flowed naturally because I'd cleared the muck and leveled up. The yoga, the retreats, Hoffman—they weren't random detours; they were tools that tuned me to a higher frequency. And the higher I climbed, the more life synced up. Looking back, it's as if the key moments in my journey light up on a map, one by one, tracing a distinct path to where I stand today.

Life as a Video Game: Facing the Villains

Here's how I see it now: life is like a video game. Each level has its villains—big challenges, looming shadows. You can dodge them, play it safe, skirmish with the small fries, collect your gold, and coast along. But you'll stay stuck, looping the same level, burning through lives until the game's over. To level up, you have to face the boss—the towering, terrifying villain. And you can't do it with weak stats. You need power-ups, high energy, the good stuff.

It's a wild, cosmic quest where you're the hero, and the goal isn't just to survive—it's to grow, to sing your unique energy's song. Each level throws the villains at you: big, daunting bosses with the pesky small fries nipping at your heels. The petty grudges, endless distractions, or emotions you shove down—are easy to skirmish with. You can dodge the big boss, fight these minions, collect shiny coins of comfort, and keep playing. But here's the catch: skirmishing drains your lives, your precious emotional energy, looping you in the same level, battling new small fries with the same old moves. Run out of lives, and you're stuck, replaying the level until you face the main villain—the raw, real emotion you've been avoiding.

The main villain isn't a monster; it's the deep feeling you need to express to grow, like grief's heavy shadow or fear's tight grip. Avoid it, and you're trapped in Maya's illusion, as we explored in Chapter 11, circling the same battles, your energy sapped by small fries like resentment or denial. To level up, you must confront the boss, but not with a splintered stick. You need power-ups—high-vibration emotions from David Hawkins' map. Shame (20) or fear (100) leave you underpowered, swinging weakly, your heart knotted. Courage (200), acceptance (350), love (500)—these are your glowing armour, your sharpened blade, filling you with the strength to triumphantly move forward.

My first villain was grief, a towering boss after Arjun's passing. I could've lingered in apathy's fog (50), skirmishing with small fries like numbness or blame, looping endlessly. Instead, I faced it, tears spilling, climbing to courage, then acceptance, my energy surging as I leveled up. The business collapse came next, a fierce foe. Pride (175) tempted me to cling to the wreckage, fighting petty battles to prove myself. With Human Design's passenger mindset, I observed, let go, and stepped into coaching with complete faith in the synchronicity that led me here, reason (400) guiding me to the next level. Each villain grew tougher, but my arsenal—tools like Enneagram, Gene Keys, and emotional awareness—grew stronger, my energy higher.

Think of it: if I'd stayed at fear, dodging the main villain, I'd be replaying old levels, battling new small fries with the same drained lives. But love, pulsing at 500, gave me the spark to face anything. Life's not about avoiding villains; it's about meeting them with enough heart to win. Every boss you conquer—every emotion you express—unlocks a new level, your purpose more clear, like a melody with all the right notes. So, grab your power-ups, face the villain, and keep playing—the game's too epic to stay stuck.

The Cosmic Symphony: Tuning into Group Energy

That first Enneagram workshop was the one that cracked my world wide open. At that workshop, mapping my 2w3—Helper with an Achiever's spark—felt like a key turning in a lock. I signed up for a Part 2, clueless about what was coming, expecting more tools like Human Design or Gene Keys for self-analysis. I got those, but something else stole the show: energy, alive and tingling in my palms, not faint but throbbing, a pulse I couldn't ignore. At first, I shrugged—what's the point of pulsing palms? But I learned to read it. It flared when the cosmos whispered, signaling a truth I needed to grasp.

At first, it felt like pushing the edges of what I once called sane. The facilitator was special, he didn't just guide us through Enneagram steps. As I clung to Type 8, my answers screaming

2, he claimed he could see our types—not a neon sign over my head, but a knowing in his gaze. "You're a 2," he said, calm and yet maddening. I wanted to bolt, but something held me, like a thread tugging my heart. Part 2 deepened my experience. That tingling became constant, a current I doubted. But resistance only amplified it, as Chapter 11 taught: what you avoid, you magnify. Lucid dreams hinted at what was next. The right people appeared, perfectly timed. I stopped fighting, questioned it along the way, but let it flow.

I dove into astrology, coaching friends with readings, not as a fortune-teller but a storyteller. I began helping clients craft narratives. My approach emerged as practical yet cosmic—using stars as a language. I noticed that leaning on logic alone weakened my readings, so I let go, speaking what came through, trusting myself as a conduit for the client's subconscious, or maybe the cosmos itself. It's not my astrology know-how; it's the message meant for them. As I embraced this role—vessel for the stars—opportunities multiplied, aligning with my Gene Key 31's Siddhi: saying what must be said, words rising from the collective, unattached to ego. That's my path, but yours may be different, carved by your unique energy, ready to shine.

What truly cracked me open at that Part 2 workshop? Group energy, the invisible force that fast-tracked my growth. We're all unique sparks, but we're also aspects of one absolute energy. When we connect, we tap into that wholeness, our auras blending like notes in a symphony. Ancient cultures knew this—group prayer, whether Vedic rituals or church gatherings, amplifies prana, lifting each soul's frequency. Alone, prayer might nudge you away from fear (100, Hawkins' scale) and toward courage (200), a spark in your aura. But in a group prayer, everyone's vibration rises, creating a collective aura pulsing higher—say, at hope (310) or love (500). It's like an invisible Network Spinal session, "clearing old silt," those conditioned kinks from childhood.

Picture an event by motivational speaker Tony Robbins, 10,000 souls chanting, moving, rallying to courage or determination—Epstein's Transform Energy, the fuel for change. The group aura surges, and you feed into it, your frequency jumping, flushing out fear or shame like a river breaking free. Religious meetings, political rallies—they do this, too, stirring hope or even anger, though often fleeting. Why fleeting? Without intent, the high fades, and the energy slips back to baseline, as I've seen in clients after highly charged events; they are energized but unchanged. This workshop paired group energy with learning—Enneagram, Human Design, Gene Keys—expanding my mind, building my intent to shift. That collective energy attuned me, my palms tingling, my 2w3's purpose made more clear.

My facilitator didn't create the symphony; he tuned us to our highest pitch, harmonizing with the cosmos. Living true to your type—your unique energy—does the same. Life brings chances to sync with others, whether in a workshop, a prayer circle, or a fleeting moment of connection. The more who join, the richer the symphony, until it's perfection itself, as Richard Rudd's 18th Gene Key dreams: a collective vision of humanity's perfection on the material plane. My Gene Key 41, my design Sun, echoes this, its gift is "attuning to the next evolutionary grid, waiting to take form". We're all moving toward a pitch-perfect world where everyone is resonating to the cosmic song we were too out of tune to hear.

This book has been a bridge, weaving spirituality with practicality, offering practical metaphysical tools to navigate life's storms with courage and clarity. But here, in this final chapter, I'm leaping off the edge—into what some might call madness, or perhaps just a wider truth. If that's not your style, dive back into the earlier chapters; their tools are grounded, tested, and effective. For the seekers, the adventurers, the gloriously cuckoo—let's peek beyond the veil together.

The Cuckoo Corner: Aliens, Eggs, and Open Minds

Now it gets wild—welcome to what I call the "cuckoo corner." I used to skip over this stuff—aliens, past lives, other dimensions. Social media's teeming with it. You've got the naive crowd chirping, "Manifest with gratitude!"—cute but thin. Then the practical ones: "Transform your life with these steps"—solid, with some substance. And then the cuckoos—aliens among us, parallel timelines, past-life regressions. I'd scroll past, smirking.

India is steeped in woo-woo for those who let it in. My roots are in Kerala, a region India hails as the land of tantra. And no, tantra isn't all about sex, despite what the West thinks. Its Sanskrit root means "to weave" or "to compose." Ancient tantric texts describe rituals—visualizations, yoga, guidance from gurus—to invoke powerful deities, promising other-worldly gifts like longevity or multi-dimensional travel alongside spiritual awakening. It is a religious mysticism, where ritual, meditation, visualization, mantra, and yogic practices are used to transcend ordinary existence and realize ultimate reality. I'm not here to praise tantra or win it fans—just to say it was within my cultural orbit, yet I'd rejected it, along with all things Hindu. Maybe tantra is the extreme, but it also raised the question in me - "what if there is more?" And the deeper I waded into this journey, the more these ideas cropped up, and I eventually stopped brushing them off.

It started with a friend who was organizing a spiritual retreat. I tagged along out of curiosity. I walked in with a buzz of intrigue but no clue what was coming, and I didn't know what to expect. But I was the intrepid seeker now, so why not dive in? The retreat promised to awaken "supernatural abilities" (or, more accurately, "intuitive superpowers") Think clairvoyance, clairsentience, clairaudience—those heightened senses that pick up vibes or insights beyond the everyday.

First, they handed us a crystal pendulum. I actually cringed when I was holding it. It felt like I'd stumbled into a cheesy New Age movie. But I went with it, swinging the pendulum as directed, trying to suss out which of these so-called superpowers might be mine. Then the facilitator sauntered over, calm and knowing, and said, "Yep, you've got the abilities." I nearly laughed out loud—it sounded ridiculous. But deep down, the competitive Nisha in me, that Enneagram 3 wing, was quietly fist-pumping!

Then came the past-life regression—an unexpected digression into a hypnotic state. Once deeply relaxed and in a flow state, I saw myself as an ordinary Indian man from some hazy slice of history. Nothing grand, just a regular guy. I emerged thinking; that was odd. Later, I swapped stories with a friend, and she hit me with a curveball: she'd seen herself as an alien during her trance state. I kept my poker face, but inside? I wondered if she was serious. Aliens and conspiracy theories belonged to the unhinged—or so I'd thought. I'd pegged her as steady, not the type to buy into the idea of extraterrestrial lives. Yet there I was, fresh from swinging a crystal pendulum like a woo-woo newbie, wondering if we'd all lost it—or if, just maybe, there was something to this madness.

Once I was home, the thought of her alien tale made me chuckle quietly. My son, Rajiv, on hearing my little outburst, asked me what was up. I shared the story, fully expecting him to laugh, too. He didn't. "You actually believe it? I asked. "Why not?" he responded, then sent me a video on Egg Theory.

The Egg Theory is a fascinating thought experiment that reimagines how all human lives are connected, with a twist: everything—every life, every moment—is happening simultaneously, not one after another. The theory proposes there's just one consciousness—yours—and it's experiencing every human life that ever was, is, or will be. These lives aren't lined up in a sequence like a playlist. Instead, they're all unfolding parallelly, right now, in a timeless "present." Forget the idea of time marching forward from past to future. Picture it as a massive web where every point—every life, every experience—exists at the same moment.

Your consciousness is like a spotlight, focusing on one thread of this web (your current life), but all the other threads (every other human or maybe alien life) are active and happening alongside yours, simultaneously. When your current life ends, your consciousness doesn't "move on" to another life. That next life is already happening in parallel. Your awareness simply shifts its focus to another thread in the web—like switching channels on a TV where all the shows are playing at once. There's no delay, no order, because all lives coexist in this timeless space. Imagine you're living your life right now, while simultaneously, you're also a farmer in ancient Egypt, a scientist in the year 3000, and a kid in a modern city. Your consciousness is tuned into one of these lifetimes at this moment. Every human experience is occurring together, layered across this vast, eternal now. The theory suggests this single consciousness is exploring every possible human experience—joy, pain, love, loss—to fully understand what it means to be human. By living all these parallel lives at once, it's gathering every piece of the puzzle, not bit by bit over time, but all in one grand, simultaneous sweep. In essence, the Egg Theory says you're not just connected to everyone—you are everyone, living every life across all of history and beyond, all at the same time. It's not about waiting to become someone else later; it's about being everyone right now, in a parallel, timeless dance of existence.

Bonkers, right? But it lodged in my mind. Well, if the concepts of time and space are only an illusion, what if my friend was/is an alien? What if I was? We are all aliens as well according to Egg Theory! Suddenly, past lives—already plausible to the Hindu in me—and even within other dimensions, didn't seem so far-fetched. My great-grandparents would've called mobile phones witchcraft, yet here we are, conversing as we face each other across oceans, with crystal clarity on screens. We accept the notion of invisible energies—Wi-Fi, radio waves—so why not consciousness rippling through time and space?

I'm still not fully convinced, but I'm not slamming the door either. And, of course, the more I opened up to new possibilities, the more extraordinary things unfolded. Synchronicities surged. Ideas flooded in. My energy shifted, and life got weirder—in a thrilling way. A wise friend once said, "What you avoid, you amplify." Maybe that's what happened to me—I'd dodged the cuckoo stuff, and it grew louder until I couldn't ignore it.

Embracing the Nonsense: A Crack in the Veil

I used to scoff readily at ideas that didn't bend to logic, but I've met much greater skeptics than myself . At a recent business event, talk turned to the Enneagram, and I lit up, sharing how my 2w3—Helper with an Achiever's spark—cracked my world open. One guy responded with anger, declaring, "It's complete bullshit, just astrology nonsense!" I clarified, "No astrology in it," but he doubled down, "It's not based on anything—pure nonsense!" His scorn stung, a jab at my logical self that left me momentarily speechless, my heart racing with unspoken defenses.

Later, I wished I'd replied, "Of course it's nonsense—and it's not." Cryptic? Maybe. I'm not chasing guru vibes, but it's true. Gary Zukav, in The Dancing Wu Li Masters, writes, "The importance of nonsense can hardly be overstated. The more clearly we experience something as 'nonsense,' the more clearly we are experiencing the boundaries of our own self-imposed cognitive structures." Enneagram seemed absurd until it shifted something in me, revealing a melody with just the right notes.

This "nonsense" opened doors to quantum mechanics, science wilder than any mystical tale. In The Dancing Wu Li

Masters, Gary Zukav offers a luminous guide to this strange realm, translating the esoteric mathematics of quantum physics into an accessible poetic narrative. Written not for physicists but for seekers of wonder, the book—with a title that evokes the masters of pattern and possibility in the Chinese term "Wu Li"—reveals quantum mechanics as a dance of probabilities. This is a dance in which the rational view expands to embrace what once seemed absurd, a concept Zukav illuminated in the above quote about the value of "nonsense." His work contrasts the clockwork predictability of Newtonian determinism—in which every event follows rigid rules—with the subatomic realm's wild possibilities, where the impossible becomes real. Quantum mechanics isn't just theory—it's a process for phenomena beyond our senses, often defying a rational grasp. As Zukav notes, "rational" now stretches to embrace what was once paradoxical or nonsensical.

Take the famous thought experiment of Schrödinger's cat; physicist Erwin Schrödinger imagined placing a cat in a sealed box along with a poisonous substance that has an equal chance of killing the cat—or not—within an hour. Schrödinger proposed that, at the end of the hour, the cat could be said to be both alive and dead, in a superposition of states until the box is opened, and that the act of observation randomly determines whether the cat is alive or dead. Schrödinger intended the example to demonstrate what he saw as the absurd nature of quantum science. Quantum theory uses the term "superposition" to describe two states coexisting at once. It defies logic. It's nonsense, yet real, and necessitates a suspension of belief, like when I was bewildered by my tingling palms in the workshop.

Consider light itself, that primal spark of creation. Light is both a particle and a wave, a duality that baffled scientists for centuries, as shown by the double-slit experiment. In this setup, particles like electrons fired one by one through two slits create an interference pattern on a screen, behaving like waves that pass through both slits at once in a state of superposition. Yet, when a detector is added to observe which slit each particle takes, the pattern collapses into simple stripes, as if the particles revert to solid form. This observer effect reveals how measurement itself alters outcomes, reminding us that science isn't absolute—reality can shift based on how we look at it. For a deeper dive, check out explanations from sources like the American Physical Society or Richard Feynman's lectures on quantum mechanics.

Now consider quantum entanglement: two particles remain linked once joined, no matter how far apart. Touch one, and the other responds instantly, as if bound by a thread across the cosmos. This feels like the Magnetic Monopole of Human Design, that inner force pulling us toward our destiny, connecting us to others in a tapestry of purpose. If science reveals such mysteries, defying the rules we thought governed reality, might it invite us to keep an open mind about spirituality, where perception shapes our path and hidden patterns guide our lives?

Enter the Many Worlds Interpretation (MWI) of quantum mechanics, a vision so bold it feels mythological. MWI suggests that when a quantum event occurs, like light choosing to act as particle or wave, or the cat's fate hanging in the balance, reality itself splits. Every possible outcome unfolds in its own universe, each as real as the one we know. The wave function, that mathematical ghost of all possibilities, never collapses—it branches. The cat lives in one universe, dies in another, and you—observer and hero—exist in both, living distinct lives, unaware of the other. Every choice, every moment, births new worlds, a cosmic kaleidoscope of realities. Countless versions of you live countless lives, each choice spawning new worlds, as real as this one.

This idea echoes the Egg Theory we explored earlier, where you are every person, a single consciousness living all lives across time, learning through each perspective to grow into wholeness. Both MWI and the Egg Theory assert that one soul is weaving a tapestry of experience. Like the group energy that I felt in my workshop, where our auras harmonized into a symphony, these countless lives—parallel or past—resonate as fragments of one absolute energy. Each life, each universe, carries emotional lessons, tuning us toward the collective perfection of Gene Key 18.

Zukav calls quantum physics "stranger than science fiction," and he's right—the subatomic is as real as the ground beneath you, yet it dances beyond reason. This quantum weirdness whispers of ideas I once readily dismissed. All the concepts shared by new age gurus that seemed utterly crazy to me before—like multiple dimensions, cosmic energy grids, or awakening hidden potentials—now seem more plausible, especially when they echo quantum principles in unexpected ways. For instance, author and hypnotherapist Dolores Cannon's tales of past lives and parallel dimensions sound like fantasy, yet the Many Worlds Interpretation of quantum mechanics suggests multiple realities could exist, each holding fragments of our greater story. Maybe like Schrödinger's Cat, we are both alive and dead until observed, capable of holding multiple states at once, giving rise to a prism of possibilities.

Author and speaker, Matias De Stefano's cosmic grids that are energy networks weaving connections between sacred sites and universal memories, feel wild, yet superposition implies that our consciousness might hold multiple layers, and that ancient wisdom is stored within our souls. His grids, like quantum entanglement's cosmic threads linking particles across vast distances, suggest that we're part of a universal web, tapping into timeless truths. Jacqueline Hobbs, also known as Oracle Girl, describes the rising planetary vibration that is waking dormant DNA codes within us. Author James Redfield's "The Celestine Prophecy" illuminates the concept of synchronicity as subtle energy exchanges that are guiding us. All these ideas feel less far-fetched when quantum mechanics is brought into view.

Quantum physics mocks our senses, yet it is true. So could these spiritual visions align with quantum truths? Maybe. As a skeptic turned believer, I hold them lightly—plausible, not proven. Science doesn't yet confirm the existence of Dolores Cannon's dimensions or Matias De Stefano's cosmic grids, but a century ago, quantum mechanics was considered nonsense, too. My journey, grounded in tools like Enneagram, Human Design and Gene Keys, keeps me tethered yet open, ready to dance with unseen possibilities. Gary Zukav declares that light has no properties independent of us: without consciousness, light doesn't exist. We're co-creators, our emotions tuning the prism through which reality forms.

This brings me back to Maya, the Hindu and Buddhist concept that is often misunderstood. When proponents of New Age thinking say, "Nothing's real, it's all Maya," folks wince, picturing something like a leap off a building with no consequences. Reality has rules—gravity keeps planets in orbit, pain signals potential harm. But Maya is the illusion veiling the ultimate unity, causing us to see separation where there's none. Buddhism calls it the false narrative of a permanent self, spun by emotions like fear or pride. Maya isn't about denying existence; it's perspective, clouded by our emotional lens, coloring reality like light through a prism. As previous chapters showed, emotions can be viewed as giving voice to the different frequencies of energy—shame (20) traps us in Maya's fog, love (500) clears it, revealing the cosmic framework.

Zukav helps to bridge this divide between the seen and unseen, noting, "Acceptance without proof is the fundamental characteristic of Western religion. Rejection without proof is the fundamental characteristic of Western science." Yet mind and heart are one. His "Wu Li Masters"—physicists dancing with mystery—presents science and faith as different rhythms in the same dance. Zukav's claim is that the key to understanding the universe is in you, and this mirrors all the ancient religious teachings. The synchronicity highlighted in Redfield's "The Celestine Prophecy," suggests that our consciousness, shaped by emotions, crafts reality. A skeptic might view all this as nonsense, but nonsense is just a crack in Maya's veil, inviting us to see from a new and expanded perspective.

Does quantum physics prove faith? Not quite, but it opens doors, whispering that reality is weirder and more connected than we dared to dream. Faith, here, isn't blind belief—it's dancing with the unknown, trusting truths beyond proof while holding space for doubt. I barely believe it all myself, and I'm not asking you to either; these ideas—from parallel worlds and cosmic grids to humanity's evolution—are just perspectives, much like the Enneagram or astrology, where a shift in method can redefine your sun sign and supposed core identity. A skeptic might call us mad for exploring such vague, nebulous territories, but the point isn't their veracity. Rather than chasing external stories, let's turn inwards, using everything as an opportunity to explore the cosmos that is within us. Ultimately, the only thing you can truly trust is your own perception—because everything else, even the greatest scientific truths, is guided or colored in some way by another's lens. It's all built on layers of interpretation, leaving no absolute truth, only what resonates as right in the moment, shaped by our inner compass. It's the attitude we bring that's important: an open mind, treating everything as tools for self-exploration and nothing more. This mindset might lead us deeper, into higher theosophical texts or Vedanta's profound inquiries. But those are learnings for another day, perhaps another book. For now, this is about embracing the human experience: recognizing that we are the source manifesting itself, seeking out experiences to understand life. These explorations are merely first steps—as we evolve, we may delve further, but the beauty, as Gary Zukav's Wu Li Masters teach, is in the dance. So let's keep moving, keep feeling, with courage, love, and peace pulsing through us, ready to embrace the mystery and meet on the other side of the veil of illusion.

The Endgame: Just Be

Here's the twist: there's no endgame to chase, no final villain or ultimate prize. Just be. Let your energy hum, let the synchronicities roll. As Ra Uru Hu, the Human Design founder said, we're passengers, not drivers. I get it now. I'm not clutching the wheel—I'm in the backseat, savoring the scenery, trusting the ride. So that's it. Clear your emotions, level up, face the villains, keep an open mind. Life's a game, a puzzle, a wild, tangled yarn. Unravel it your way—just don't shy away from peeking beyond the veil.

REFERENCES

Auel, Jean M. The Clan of the Cave Bear. New York: Crown Publishing Group, 1980.

Blanks, Richard H., Tonya L. Schuster, and Donald M. Epstein. "A Retrospective Assessment of Network Care Using a Survey of Self-Reported Health and Wellness." Journal of Vertebral Subluxation Research 1, no. 4 (1997): 11–27.

Bunnell, Lynda. The Definitive Book of Human Design: The Science of Differentiation. Encinitas, CA: Jovian Archive Press, 2011.

Cannon, Dolores. The Convoluted Universe: Book One. Huntsville, AR: Ozark Mountain Publishing, 2001.

De Stefano, Matías. Initiation. Gaia TV, 2020–present.

Emoto, Masaru. The Hidden Messages in Water. Translated by David A. Thayne. Hillsboro, OR: Beyond Words Publishing, 2004.

Epstein, Donald M. The 12 Stages of Healing: A Network Approach to Wholeness. Deerfield Beach, FL: Health Communications, 1994.

Epstein, Donald M. The Seeker's Code: Your Access to the Spiritual Universe. Boulder, CO: Donald Epstein Publishing, 2002.

Epstein, Donald M., Simon Senzon, and Daniel Lemberger. "Network Spinal Analysis and Evidence-Based Care: Association with Self-Reported Improvements in Wellness and Quality of Life." Journal of Alternative and Complementary Medicine 22, no. 7 (2016): 544–556. https://doi.org/10.1089/acm.2016.0031.

Everett, Hugh III. "Relative State Formulation of Quantum Mechanics." Reviews of Modern Physics 29, no. 3 (1957): 454–462. https://doi.org/10.1103/RevModPhys.29.454.

Forrest, Steven. The Inner Sky: How to Make Wiser Choices for a More Fulfilling Life. San Diego, CA: ACS Publications, 1984.

Freud, Sigmund. The Ego and the Id. 1923. Reprint, New York: W. W. Norton & Company, 1960.

Goodman, Linda. Love Signs: A New Approach to the Human Heart. New York: Harper & Row, 1978.

Greene, Liz. Relating: An Astrological Guide to Living with Others on a Small Planet. London: Coventure, 1977.

Greene, Liz. The Astrology of Fate. York Beach, ME: Weiser Books, 1984.

Hand, Robert. Planets in Transit: Life Cycles for Living. Atglen, PA: Whitford Press, 1976.

Hawkins, David R. Power vs. Force: The Hidden Determinants of Human Behavior. Sedona, AZ: Veritas Publishing, 1995.

Hawkins, David R. Letting Go: The Pathway of Surrender. Carlsbad, CA: Hay House, 2012.

Heron, Heidi, and Laureli Blyth. 30 Days to NLP: Transform Your Life One Day at a Time. London: Crown House Publishing, 2012.

Hobbs, Jacqueline (Oracle Girl). Official Teachings and Writings. https://www.oraclegirl.org.

Hoffman Institute. The Hoffman Process. San Rafael, CA: Hoffman Institute International, 2004.

Kajita, Takaaki, and Arthur B. McDonald. "Neutrino Oscillations and the Nobel Prize in Physics 2015." Physics World. Accessed October 9, 2025. http://hitoshi.berkeley.edu/neutrino/PhysicsWorld.pdf.

Lipton, Bruce H. The Biology of Belief: Unleashing the Power of Consciousness, Matter, and Miracles. Carlsbad, CA: Hay House, 2005.

Maté, Gabor, with Daniel Maté. The Myth of Normal: Trauma, Illness, and Healing in a Toxic Culture. New York: Avery, 2022.

Miller, George A. "The Magical Number Seven, Plus or Minus Two: Some Limits on Our Capacity for Processing Information." Psychological Review 63, no. 2 (1956): 81–97. https://doi.org/10.1037/h0043158.

Pauli, Wolfgang. "Letter on the Hypothesis of the Neutron (1931)." Accessed October 9, 2025. https://icecube.wisc.edu/neutrino-history/1931/01/1931-pauli-presents-hypothetical-neutron-particle/.

Pert, Candace B. Molecules of Emotion: Why You Feel the Way You Feel. New York: Scribner, 1997.

Redfield, James. The Celestine Prophecy: An Adventure. New York: Warner Books, 1993.

Riso, Don Richard, and Russ Hudson. 1999. The Wisdom of the Enneagram: The Complete Guide to Psychological and Spiritual Growth for the Nine Personality Types. New York: Bantam Books.

Rudd, Richard. Gene Keys: Unlocking the Higher Purpose Hidden in Your DNA. London: Watkins Publishing, 2013.

Rudd, Richard. The Gene Keys: Embracing Your Higher Purpose. London: Watkins Media, 2015.

Rudd, Richard. The Gene Keys Golden Path: Volume 1, The Activation Sequence. Dev Aura, UK: Gene Keys Publishing, 2012.

Rudd, Richard. The Gene Keys Golden Path: Volume 2, The Venus Sequence. Dev Aura, UK: Gene Keys Publishing, 2015.

Rudd, Richard. The Gene Keys Golden Path: Volume 3, The Pearl Sequence. Dev Aura, UK: Gene Keys Publishing, 2016.

Vivekananda, Swami. Raja Yoga: Being Lectures on Raja Yoga with Patanjali's Aphorisms and Commentaries. New edition. New York: Brentano's, 1920.

Weir, Andy. The Egg and Other Stories. Lexington, KY: CreateSpace Independent Publishing Platform, 2015.

Zukav, Gary. The Dancing Wu Li Masters: An Overview of the New Physics. New York: William Morrow, 1979.

Zukav, Gary. The Seat of the Soul. New York: Simon & Schuster, 1989.